T0299482

Dear Dad

Dear Dad

Edited by
SAMUEL JOHNSON OAM

Illustrated by
SHAUN TAN

 hachette
AUSTRALIA

hachette
AUSTRALIA

Published in Australia and New Zealand in 2019
by Hachette Australia
(an imprint of Hachette Australia Pty Limited)
Level 17, 207 Kent Street, Sydney NSW 2000
www.hachette.com.au

10 9 8 7 6 5 4 3 2 1

A catalogue record for this
book is available from the
National Library of Australia

ISBN: 978 0 7336 4314 9 (hardback)

Cover and internal design by Christabella Designs
Cover and internal illustrations by Shaun Tan
Typeset in Garamond Regular by Kirby Jones
Printed and bound in Australia by McPherson's Printing Group

The paper this book is printed on is certified against the
Forest Stewardship Council® Standards. McPherson's
Printing Group holds FSC® chain of custody certification
SA-COC-005379. FSC® promotes environmentally
responsible, socially beneficial and economically viable
management of the world's forests.

Contents

A message from the editor

A letter that begins with the words 'Dear Dad' is as intimate as it gets, each one as unique as the dads themselves, and the kids they raised (or didn't). They share excitements, secrets, regrets, treasured memories and dreams, carefully committed to paper for dads' eyes only, whether they're still with us or long gone.

So many are never written, the thoughts to and about our dads often left unsaid. Until now!

I asked Australia's most notorious and best-loved notables to each write a letter to their dad, or a dad-like dad, in the name of cancer vanquishment. None of them were paid for their work, so that more profits from the sale of this book can be spent on medical research. To each author, thank you.

Samuel Johnson OAM

Dear Dad

Of course, a note. You were the best at notes. Letters were too earnest for you, too schmaltzy. You wrote notes. Like that one you sent me that sits bound in sticky tape above my hard drive. The last one. The Last Note. Sounds like a bloody thriller title, one of those door-stopping pulp-fiction paperbacks you were always reading. The last note. That killer line you left me with that always gets me all wet-eyed and longing: 'You have done all the right things.' I use that on my girls. You have done all the right things. Not all the spectacular things. Not all the showy things. *Just the right things.*

Beth finished primary school this year and she's excited about high school, and you would have lost your shit, Dad, last Friday, when the principal handed her the hallowed 'Spirit of the School' award. The things they said about her. The right things. Never the girl who gets the spotlight, never the showy kid. Just the quiet kid who cares a great deal about a great many things. And you know who was happiest for her? It was Sylvie. Nine-year-old cyclone Sylvie, who, you'd probably be secretly happy to know, is still not quite as possessed by the spirit of Catholic saints as she is, like you, by the spirit of Keith Richards.

I did end up writing that book I told you about. I called it *Boy Swallows Universe*. That title's a newspaper headline, but it means what it says. Swallow it all, right? The good stuff, the bad stuff, the beautiful stuff, the mad stuff. You taught me that. Swallow it down then cough it back up as words. Surprise everybody. It's all in there: Mum, you, the boys, Slim, that feller, that other feller and, yep, him too.

A fair few people liked the book, Dad. I see them reading it across Australia and they're enjoying themselves. You're making them laugh and you're making them cry, and every time I see that book on a shelf somewhere I think about how much you'd have loved that sight. Maybe you can see it. I wrote it for you, Dad. That's my gift to you this Father's Day. Not a bathroom towel. Not a jam-jar grip. A story. A love story where you're a central character. You still are that central character. You always will be. Happy Father's Day, Dad, and thanks for all of it. You did all the right things.

Trent

Trent Dalton: four-time ABIA award winner, multi Walkley award winner

Dear Dad

One day when I was about eight or nine, I was sitting at our family table (the rectangular one you swapped the round one for) and I rather thoughtlessly mentioned that I was bored. You bristled and then your ears went hot red. You glared at me with that look that said, 'Don't you dare look elsewhere!' Your lip curled. Your eyebrows were tight. Your contempt and your fury jostled for position. Eventually you said, very calmly, very intently, way too politely ... '*Bored*, are you?'

I gambled well on this being rhetorical and you stormed off into your study. I didn't move. After some loud noises you seethed back to me, hiding something behind your back. I had time to wonder whether it was your belt. You slammed a pad of paper down on the table in front of me as hard as you could. It made a huge sound and the table nearly broke. I was terrified. This was a new level. Out of nowhere, you slammed a pen down just as hard, frightening me equally. You stood back over my shoulder. I couldn't see you, and you spoke calmly, very measured, sickly polite.

'On that piece of paper you will write down ten things – no, let's make it twenty things – that don't cost any money, that would *alleviate* your *boredom*. Give me an example.'

I fumbled through my mind nervously for an acceptable answer. 'I could read a book?'

'Excellent! What else?'

'I could ride my bike?'

'Fantastic, now don't move off that chair until you finish the list, then call me.'

It wasn't a hard list to fill, once I thought about it. I triple-checked the list before calling for you in my chastened voice. You came back into the room without all the bluster. You ordered me to read the list out to you.

Then you leant down and put all your weight into your words … '*Now fucking pick one!* And *then*, if you get *bored* doing that, I dunno, how about you *pick another one!*'

Needless to say, I spent the rest of the day choosing from my list and doing stuff. I remember you kissing me goodnight in your study that night. As I was walking away you called after me … 'I hope you don't grow up to be a boring person.'

I'm writing to thank you, Dad. I've remained curious since that day, and that curiosity you fostered in me has, all these years later, propelled me beyond my wildest aspirations. Your many other wisdoms endure, too, and I remain gratefully yours,

Mister Happy

Sammy Seal

Samuel Johnson OAM: Dancing with the Stars *winner, BOOM*

Dear Dad

Thank you for the twenty-four-hour rule.

I remember rabbiting on about something that turned out to be inconsequential from atop my high horse one day while you sat there with your legs crossed in a state of equanimity. When my rant ran out, I asked your thoughts on potential solutions to this life-altering issue.

'Wait twenty-four hours before you respond.'

This solution did not appeal to me.

You went on to say that mobiles and emails were too instant; that people reacted too quickly and too emotionally when in fact time cures most ill wills. And if it didn't, measured responses made for smoother roads.

'What if I'm still as upset tomorrow?' I asked with the certainty that I would feel just as slighted, if not more, the following day.

'Then wait another twenty-four hours.'

The twenty-four-hour rule has served me well for many years, and I have paid it forward.

Recently I walked out to the back porch. Your grandsons were sitting there, talking with youthful urgency. They were debating how to respond to an offensive SMS, and whether or not they should even be friends with the person at all. After going around in widening circles, one stopped and said, 'Twenty-four-hour rule.' They fist-bumped, visibly relaxed and I slipped back inside unseen.

Job done, Dad.

Hilde

Hilde Hinton: author, prison officer and the Other Sister at Love Your Sister

Dear dads of children with rare diseases

To each of you, I am in awe of your commitment and unconditional love for your child. Always on call, 24 hours each and every day of the year.

Your child has an incredible story to tell, interwoven with sadness, elation, frustration, hope, despair and unwavering determination.

I see the commitment in your eyes, hear the resolution in your voice, and feel your hopes and belief. Nothing is too big or too small for you to provide. You share the bread-winning duties, and the pain. Mostly you are the rock, with little time for yourself, if any at all. You are the provider of security, confidence and inspiration, proud of the memories your family build together.

Patience is your friend, when time might be against you, always keeping everyone calm in stressful situations. Your connection and unwavering love enables you to observe and realise the hidden communication in the hands, or the smile, the sheer delight of a laugh or two, the mischievous streak and a sense of humour. Your reward is that beautiful smile, the sparkle in their eye, just one small step taken.

You reach out with humility and no expectation. You endure unfathomable challenges every day, with no respite or finish line. I'm constantly amazed by your indomitable spirit and uplifting attitude that conquers obstacles most of us never have to confront. Courage and strength of character have always inspired me. Rising to the occasion and never giving up come from a resolute will, where determination, effort and belief come together.

Our focus is their wellbeing and the difference we can make to their lives – to help them not only thrive, but in many instances survive.

No one should ever have to stand alone; everyone needs a team to support them.

Always 100 per cent.

Steve

Steve Waugh: cricketing legend

Dear Dad

This is my seventh fatherless Father's Day, but I'm still not over missing you. You died so unexpectedly, from blood clots. Despite the fact that I was a 53-year-old mother of two, I felt like a little orphan girl. Grief, of course, is the price we pay for love. But what niggles me is guilt. Did you ever know just how much I appreciated you?

When I tell people about you, I talk about your kindness, your cleverness, your twinkly-eyed wit and warmth. I also confess how my three sisters and I made fun of your name, 'Mervyn'. As you laid most of Australia's optic fibre, we nicknamed you 'Optic Merv'.

I tell them how in your youth you were a famous Rugby League player for the Bulldogs. Mum still displays the newspaper clippings, with your handsome face emblazoned across the front pages, mid-tackle. For a time, you were the fastest front-row forward in Australian history.

You won a hundred pounds in a race at the Sydney Cricket Ground, with which you bought a second-hand Standard car.

It was always in need of repair. Mum recalls how she'd have to alight, babe in arms, to trudge up every hill, as you could only ascend in reverse, smoke billowing.

As a Rugby League star, what you wanted was four boys whom you could train to scrum and run ... What you got instead were four feisty daughters.

I suspect all teenage daughters take their dads for granted. For many years you were just the nocturnal, suited and booted creature who vanished in the early morning and only reappeared at night. Habits included putting out the garbage, untangling the pool sweep, and brewing your own beer, which occasionally exploded. You were also the recipient of all those strange envelopes with cellophane windows ...

To us four sassy, busy, boisterous girls, you were just the tall, muscular figure who could hot-wire the car when we'd lost the keys at the beach, save us from cockroaches/mice/floods/bushfires and catch the pet snake which had escaped *yet again* from my sister Jenny's bedroom and was lurking somewhere in the living room. (Mum maintains that owning a snake is a sure-fire way of avoiding wrinkles, as you will never laugh, smile or even vaguely relax ever again. Especially when the rat bought to feed the snake escapes. The *pregnant* rat ...)

You were also expert at spider disposal. Our house in Sydney's Sutherland shire was surrounded by bush. Tarantulas the size of cattle dogs were a regularity. My terrified screams demanding emergency SWAT response teams could be heard in Antarctic scientific base camps. But you could deal with the scariest of creatures with a quick and simple thwack of a tea towel.

You weren't even fazed by the kind of dogs that could drag a girl into the Underworld and use you as a chew toy. 'He's just playing,' you'd say, prising free my littlest sister, Cara, from between foaming incisors. 'Satan, down boy.'

You were always our hero – the head that was furthest out in the sea, bobbing through the breakers before surfing to shore like a human hydrofoil. The one we sent downstairs to hit the cat burglar over the head with the breadboard. The one to go out to get my sister Liz's asthma medicine from the all-night pharmacist twenty miles away, at three in the morning in the pouring rain. The adventurer who whisked us off on trips to Coolangatta, Cobar, Cooma, and even around the world in a campervan during your long service leave. The one who took all the film footage of the family – but was never in any of it; just your voice-over, telling us the exact exchange rate compared to yesterday or the gradient of the nearest railway line. You could even find the square root of the hypotenuse. (Hell, I hadn't even realised it was lost!)

Even though you were our rock and our protector and knew we loved you dearly, we cheeky daughters were more focused on your quirks than your amazing qualities. Your obsession with tractors amused us greatly. We also teased you endlessly about your fixation on petrol coupons. And nails. We were trained never to walk past a nail without stooping down to pick it up, *just in case*. We now have a nail collection big enough to rebuild Noah's Ark, if the opportunity arises. And you never left the house unless armed with superglue, DW40 and electrical tape.

Aussie dads of your vintage tend to demonstrate their love through actions. After we four girls left home, whenever we popped back for a visit, our fan belts would be tightened, tyres pumped, gauge pressures checked, oil changed, and there'd suddenly be new contact points in the distributor and fresh oil in the differential (whatever the devil that is; it's still all Swahili to me, Dad). And when you asked me how many miles I was getting to the gallon – it was the equivalent of a Shakespearean love sonnet.

After we all married and had families of our own, whenever a fuse needed changing or a digital stereo needed mending or a tax return needed filing or the car needed tuning, our mental Gregory's was open, the streets mapped and marked – with all roads leading to you, Dad. Is it any wonder we feel so lost without you?

You were immensely proud of all your eight grandchildren, all of whom excel at sport and also show a healthy interest in the toolbox. Although you were too sensible to ever wear them, it's obviously a case of Designer Genes.

Darling Dad, you touched so many lives. Whenever I watch TV or surf the web, I think of you, Optic Merv, because you're the man who helped it happen. And every Father's Day, I remind my pals to hug their own darling dads. Because oh, how I wish I could.

Love,

Kathy xxx

Kathy Lette: bestselling author

Dear Dad

It started with the great unknown. There was never any doubt, fear or questions from the moment I entered the world. How much would the inability to walk affect my ability to live? You only ever gave me hope and belief.

You taught me what it is to be a man. That the value of your word is the most valuable asset. That the loudest voice is often the weakest.

The lessons I learnt often came across without words. I learnt from your deeds and your actions. It's like I was building a compass within, and you were supplying not only the materials but pointing the direction towards north.

Forever I will be confused between your voice and my own inner monologue, reminding me to do today's job to the best of my ability and not to push today's worries into tomorrow.

But above all you taught me that family is everything. It took hearing the cries of my own child to know the pain that my tears would have caused you. But you carried those tears and moments as you carried me through my childhood.

I know when you read this, you'll note that I have exceeded the usual extent of my verbal expression. But I thought that writing 'Dear Dad, you did alright, ol' fella' wasn't quite up to it.

Love ya Dad,

Kurt

Kurt Fearnley: gold medal-winning racer, crawled the Kokoda Track

Dear Dad

It isn't easy to quantify the great outcome our family has enjoyed as a result of you leaving Scotland in the sixties, but I do know that our lives would have been vastly different if we had stayed in Glasgow. For you it was a chance to breathe after having to work three jobs just to keep the whole boat afloat.

At this point, Mum deserves to be acknowledged for refusing to go to Canada. She correctly stated that it was too cold. You kept on longing for a chance to start a new life for your family, and eventually we came to the Lucky Country.

I remember the last thing you said to me … 'I'm going to the twenty-four-hour bar, schooners all day and all night.'

I hope the schooners are still flowing, and say goodnight to Mum for me. All my love, your number-one son,

John

John Paul Young: pop legend and ARIA Hall of Fame inductee

Dear Dad

In less than a week you'll step into your best role yet. A grandfather.

You told me the other day that you were excited, but you also said, in your trying-not-to-be-too-sentimental way, that it's been a little hard to get your head around; that for the last 32 years I've been your little girl and so you've had to do some letting go.

I get it. I've had to do some letting go myself over these past nine months ... and some growing up. But mostly I've had to think about the kind of mum I want to be, the lessons I want Zan to learn and the kind of values I want to impart. Which, funnily enough, all seem to come back to you.

You taught me about fairness and humility. You taught me that money, status and power, although aspirational, don't define a person; that it's in their character, their values, their generosity. You taught me to appreciate the simple things in life, to make my bed every day and never to take things for granted. You taught me not to live life in fear and avoidance, to show up for my family and that it's good to push myself and absolutely fine to fail.

But most of all, thanks to your terrible dad jokes and ability to laugh at yourself, you taught me how to be silly. So when life starts to feel heavy, I'm reminded that it's also to be enjoyed.

Can't thank you enough for these lessons, and can't wait for you to meet your grandson.

Your little girl forever,

Tildy X

Matilda Brown: writer, director, actor, best known for her work in Lessons from the Grave *opposite her father, Bryan Brown*

Dear Dad

I blame you. You did this. I wouldn't be one of them if it weren't for you. None of us would. It's your fault. Absolutely and scientifically.

Every time I tell anyone I am one of six daughters I get the same response: Five sisters? No boys? Only girls? Six girls?! Your poor Dad!

My poor Dad?! It's your fault! The male parent determines the sex of the child. It's the sperm that carries the X or Y chromosome, and since your sperm insisted on carrying only X chromosomes to Mum's X chromosomes, the only outcome was XX – aka six baby girls! I mean, honestly, who even cares about sex when we now understand that gender is fluid and more a social construct. I digress.

My point is, I rightfully blame you. I blame you for partnering up with the biggest and most beautiful quirk burger I've ever met. I blame you for the five sisters and their unrelenting friendship that I have had to endure. I blame you for ruining my chances of a relationship with realistic expectations, because my first example of men was someone so kind he improvised original bedtime stories every night and wrapped my feet in warm towels on winter evenings.

I blame you for my sense of humour and my love of people and their stories, and for any success I have in the weird and wonderful world I work in because you (literally) put my name in lights before anyone else knew who I was.

My greatest honour is being one of Louie Youssef's girls. You did this. I wouldn't be one of them if it weren't for you. None of us would. It's your fault. Absolutely and scientifically.

Love,

Your Susie x

PS Sorry for talking about your sperm.

Susie Youssef: comedian and TV regular

Dear Dad

Thought I'd drop you a note and give you an update on what has been happening since 1992.

Sue and I had another baby. A little brother for Casey. We named him Max, not just because Max Mannix sounds cool (which it does) but because Max was the name of the guy who taught you to play guitar. You playing guitar – and the Beatles – inspired Chris and me to learn it as well. Max was also the name of the character I played in my first acting job, in *The Flying Doctors*.

Max's middle name is Elvis. He was born on Mother's Day 1993. That, coupled with buying a house and Essendon winning the flag, made for a pretty good year. You would love Max.

Sue and I finally got married in 1994. I wish you could have been there. We have been together now for 34 years and are still very much in love.

Casey was just a toddler last time you saw her. She is now 29, taller than Sue and me, and drop-dead gorgeous, even if I do say so myself. She is a better singer than me, and a great dancer and actor. She has a boyfriend called Josh who is a really nice guy. I like him.

Max is 25 and six feet tall. I don't know how that happened. If he didn't look so much like me, I'd be asking questions. He recently graduated from uni and is now a qualified counsellor. He is gay. Just joking, he is going out with a lovely girl named Sarah. I am so proud of both of my kids.

Having kids has made me realise what a wonderful dad you were. I also find myself saying the same things you said to me, like, 'If you are not using the room, turn the light off.'

There is not a day goes by that I don't think of you. I really appreciate all you did for me. The lessons learned have served me well, and I can still hear your dry sense of humour – which I have ripped off and seem to have passed on to Casey and Max.

Chris and Debby are well and now live in a fantastic house. He really stepped up when you left and continues to be a great big brother.

You were taken too soon. Sixty-four is not old, especially today. At the time, Chris and I felt ripped off. Over the years I have learned not to be sad that you aren't here, but grateful for the years you were. The memory of you, your actions, advice, love and humour live strong in my mind and actions. Thank you! With much love,

Brian

PS I'll tell you the rest when I get there. Say hi to Johnny Cash for me.

Brian Mannix: Uncanny X-Man

Dear Dad

Sorry for the delay with this letter; I have been quite busy, and of course you have been … well, dead, for quite a while. I've always wanted to tell you how much I enjoyed being your son.

As you know, I left the family home at nineteen and forged a career in show business, mainly as a singer, with a few diversions along the way. Consequently, we didn't have much time together as man to man, and you always referred to my choice of music as 'bash bash thump thump, tuneless, flaming jungle music' – a typical Yorkshireman critique. I was not offended by this and indeed enjoyed your knowledge of Italian operatic arias (to which I still listen, but don't tell anyone).

Thanks also for your sense of humour, which I cherished then and now. Thanks, Harry. Lots of love,

Glenn

Glenn Shorrock: double inductee into the ARIA Hall of Fame, as a member of The Little River Band and as a solo artist

Dear Dad

There are so many things this letter could be.

It could be an apology. I could tell you I was sorry for lots of stuff. I'd certainly apologise for all the bullshit I dished out to you as a teenager. Ugh. Yeah, that'd definitely be top of the list. So. Many. Lies!

This letter could be congratulatory. A way to express great praise for all your incredible achievements as a man, and to tell you how sincerely proud I am of you.

This could be a fuck-you letter. Like everyone, you aren't perfect, and there have been many moments in my life when I've wanted to yell at you JUST how imperfect you are.

It could be a coming-of-age revelatory letter. About the moment when I finally took you off the parent-pedestal and realised you were just a person doing your best, going through all the same stuff as everyone else in the world.

It could definitely be a thank you letter. For all the sacrifices you made to raise us kids. I'd absolutely thank you for the effort you've put in to opening up and letting me in. I know as an Englishman it can be challenging, but it means so much to me when you tell me you love me and I've made you proud.

This could be a letter of questions. Why do you get so furious at technology? Do you think I'm good at my job? Will you please reveal the secret ingredient in your gravy?

But actually, this is a letter of wishes. One wish, really. One thing I wish for you:

Put yourself first now. I'd love for you to ask yourself what YOU want, and know that it's not being selfish. It's okay for you to do stuff just for you.

But I'm not sure you ever have. I know it brings you joy and comfort to make others happy, and that's a beautiful thing, but I want you to have YOUR heart's desires too. And so does everyone who loves you.

So. Dad. What do you want for your life? Just for you? (Nothing work-related – yes, there are rules.)

Go for it with everything you have; you have my full support. I cannot wait to see what comes ...

I love you,

Michala xxx

PS Is this an appropriate forum to ask you to get your hearing checked? I've wanted to broach the subject in person many times, but thought you'd get mad. Actually, I suspect doing it this way will have the same result. (Please add this to the list of stuff I owe you an apology for.) And please consider hearing aids. Thanks, Dad. Love you!

Michala Banas: Australia's favourite Upper Middle Bogan

Dear Dad

Yes it's me. I bet you're surprised to hear from me. Didn't think I'd write, eh? It's been a while, to say the least. But it's not like I haven't thought about it.

I've still got your tools in the shed. They make me laugh, some of those old tools – even the ones you repaired – they still work! People don't do that any more. When something breaks they throw it away and buy a new one.

How is it there, anyway? You know Mum misses you. Well, we all do. Especially at family gatherings – that's the hardest for Mum. She gets teary and asks why you're not there. And your brother George, yeah – he's been smoking since you left.

I haven't dreamt of you for a while now. But the last time I did, you looked fit. I was in that awful place and you were leading me, carrying my guitars to the car. Remember? You got me sorted and out of there. Thanks for your help, Dad.

Neil

Neil Murray: songwriter, 'My Island Home'

Dear Dad

When I left home at seventeen I had stars in my eyes. I had no idea how tough life was going to be. I had no idea that decades later I'd still be looking for that elusive break as an actor.

You packed up my Holden Calais with me, drove me down to Sydney and flew back to Brisbane. You must have been so worried. But it was time to let your son go.

I've lived away since then, and I've made a whole bunch of mistakes. I barely ever got it right. I struggled; I developed crippling anxiety that consumed me for over a decade, which I'm only just starting to climb my way out of.

I've won AFIs and Logies. I've seen myself on the big screen many times. I've dabbled in the upper echelons of film, working alongside the likes of Brad Pitt. I've tasted success; but I've also lived the debilitating lows. I've been unemployed; I've lived on the smell of an oily rag.

I look back now on the times you struggled to support the family on a meagre bricklayer's wage. When I wanted to play Rugby League and there was no club for me to play, you started a club, the Browns Plains Bears, and you built the clubhouse with your own hands. When I wanted to be an actor, you found me classes and told me to dream big.

Through all this, I've never lacked faith in myself. I've never considered another path for myself. And I've never felt anything but support and love from you.

I once wanted to come home with my tail between my legs, and asked you if I could lay bricks with you. You said to me, 'I didn't lay bricks so you would have to.' Even though you would have rather had me beside you, you knew my soul would tear apart if I didn't chase my dreams.

You'll probably never understand just how much you have been the backbone of my life. When I was down, you were up. When I was successful, you were proud. When I was destitute, you helped me get by. I would not have handled the successes with humility and I would not have braved the lows with grace and determination if I hadn't known you were there.

I haven't yet made my first million, which means you haven't yet got that Group A Commodore I promised you. But I swear to you, I don't care what it takes, when it happens, you are getting that damn car, even though by the time I get around to it, it will be 50 years old and completely what you don't want. It's my point of pride. I often think about it. Of sneaking the old bomb onto your driveway, wrapping a ridiculous oversized ribbon around it, and watching the relief on your face when you see it and realise you don't have to worry about me any more.

Money isn't the measure of success, I know that. But fuck I love the symbolism of making good on my promise, and making good on the foundation you laid out before me.

And if I never get there, it's been an awesome ride. When we are both on the other side, we can ride in that V8 beast together.

The great news is I have two sons of my own. And I'm raising them as you raised me: to be free, to be themselves, to expect to work hard, and above all, to treat people with respect and dignity.

We are here but a fleeting minute, but the impact we have can last generations.

You're a brighter star than I'll ever be.

Your son,

Tony

Anthony Hayes: Logie and AACTA award-winning actor, writer, producer and director (failed theatre performer in high school)

Dear Dad

Father's Day this year will be my second without you. We lost you at 8.10 pm on 17 August last year. My beautiful and devoted mother, your partner of 55 years, and your kids were all with you, holding you, comforting you, talking to you and telling you exactly how much you meant to us.

You were our everything. You checked out in a cocoon of love, with abundant dignity. You went out on your terms. Just how you wanted to go.

I knew you, my best mate, were deteriorating. You had dementia. You still had all your marbles, but you were slowing up pretty fast. This was the most beautiful part about you passing away when you did – for as hard as it was saying goodbye, you knew exactly what was going on. The marbles in your bag may have been a bit chipped and worn, but they were all there.

After your diagnosis I set about writing a letter to you on a flight from Perth to Melbourne on 4 December. I finished the letter on 23 December and presented it to you for Christmas.

I wrote down, in no particular order, everything I loved about you, admired about you, cherished about you, respected about you. All of the great lessons I learned from you. All of the times we got into trouble together. The incredible times we shared over the journey of my life with you, right up until the end. I just kept remembering things and writing them down.

As a young fella I always thought that I would do this. Write a letter to you before you died. Now I was doing it.

When people tell me a parent of theirs is not well, I mention what I did for you. I urge them not to wait another day.

I guess, upon reflection, that letter was as much for me as it was for you, Snowy. I would be living in regret if I had not written it.

Love,

Danny

Danny 'The Green Machine' Green: retired former triple-world-champion boxer

Dear Dad

It's hard to know what to write, since you are not here.

Thanks for always being there for me and my brothers and for teaching us the rights and the wrongs of the world. To be loyal, to be a friend, to protect those you love and to never lose sight of what is most important, family.

I wish I could say this to you face to face.

I also want to thank you for teaching us kids about the land, how it affects us all and why it is so important to everyone. Your grandkids are growing up very fast and you would be proud of them, just like I am.

Most of all, thank you for teaching us what being a real man is: kind, loving, forgiving and accepting ... thank you!

Miss you, Dad, and always will!

Shannon

Shannon Noll: chart-topping, sheep-shearing Australian Idol

Dear Dad

I know it must seem strange that I have chosen to write to you instead of just picking up the phone and calling you. But I feel it is best that I write my thoughts down so that you don't interrupt me with comments such as, 'Well, that's just bloody ridiculous, son', or, 'Have you been smoking something, boy?', or, your old-time favourite, 'Remember I brought you into this world so I can take you out of it.'

All that said, here I go.

What I have come to realise since becoming a father is that I am pretty sure that no fathers throughout history actually had a clue what they were doing. I am not for a moment saying dads don't care, or that they don't try their best to be good parents. I am only stating what I believe to be true, and that is that dads don't actually know if what they are telling their children will work, help or even if it is the correct information. Let me explain how I came to this devastating realisation.

I recently found myself saying to the kids, 'Don't worry, things have a way of working out in the end,' then moments later, 'How are you supposed to learn things if I help you do your homework?' The truth was I had no idea how to do the Grade Four maths equation.

Next thing I know I am throwing around sentences like, 'Ask ya mother', 'Don't ask me how to spell it, look it up in a dictionary yourself' and, 'Well, you need to figure that one out on ya own.'

All of these comments (when I had no idea how to answer their questions) in no way gave my kids comfort or led them in any direction other than away from me.

I obviously understand how hard being a dad is, but it would have been handy to have been told at some point before becoming a dad, 'Oh son, by the way, it's a bit of a fly-by-the-seat-of-your-pants type of deal, the whole dad thing', or even just, 'There is no way of knowing if you are doing the right thing, just do ya best.'

Any information or advice like this would have let me off the hook a bit, or at least helped me realise that I am not alone with the whole 'What the hell am I supposed to do now that I am a dad' question.

I often don't know the correct advice to give children who at a very young, fragile and delicate age seem to only seek their advice from me and their mother. And when their mother isn't around, they assume that I will have all the answers to absolutely everything.

So, Dad, I write to you today not to complain about the way you raised me, but to say that it just would have been nice to know that being a dad is a bit like playing battleships and cruisers, you just yell out a few guesses and wait to find out if they were hits or misses.

I do want to say that I love you to bits, Dad, and my kids seem to love me too, so you obviously did a great job of being a dad to me and I am going okay so far as well.

That's all I wanted to say, Dad. I'll see you Saturday at the kids' footy.

Love your son and your grandchildren's dad,

Shane

PS Thanks for being there for me, Dad, which is my favourite thing you do, to be honest … always being there for me.

Shane Jacobson: song and dance man, author, screenwriter, creative director, producer, motorsport enthusiast

Dear Dad

Words left unspoken because there is never enough time. Lessons to learn but there is never enough time.

Dad, you taught me to believe in myself. To express myself without fear. You also taught me to be open to different opinions, to listen to others, because quite possibly their knowledge might change how I feel. This is what I hold dear: that a conversation or difference of opinion is not an argument, it is a chance to learn. I've often heard the phrase, 'Never talk politics, race or religion', but if we all followed your lesson to me, these discussions would be opportunities to learn and to impart knowledge, and I can't see any losers in that.

You taught me equality. That no minority should have to strive to achieve it, because it is every human's right to be considered equal. You never had to say it, but I learned from you that racism shouldn't be a word; it just shouldn't exist.

I learned that respect is not a given but is earned, and that principle has become the basis for every day of my life. You taught me that we reap what we sow, that we are all individuals and that that is the blessing of existing.

Dad, with your many faults, you taught me we all have them, and it's what we learn from our mistakes that matters. I wasn't proud of all your decisions, and you allowed me to express this to you. I loved you all the more for letting me tell you exactly how I felt.

You taught me to embrace my individuality and to parent my children the same way. When it was time for you to go I know how proud you felt that I had succeeded in parenting truly individual children.

But in the end, the greatest lesson you taught me was to love passionately and be steadfast. You and Mum may not have stayed together, and your mistakes were momentous and life-changing for many. But Dad, you didn't sway from making sure I knew I was born out of love, and for a child, that is everything. I thank you for a gift that money can't buy, so that I could do the same for your legacy, your grandchildren.

Cassandra

Cassandra Thorburn: teacher, children's author, journalist, television producer, Dancing with the Stars *contestant*

Dear Dad

You've been gone 46 years now. I wonder how much more life you'd have lived if the treatments available today for your heart condition had been available then.

My biggest disappointment is that I think we were finally becoming really close. I'm sure you'd have been enormously proud of all of your grandchildren and, now, great-grandkids. It's amazing, though, when I look at the young ones in our family, how much I see of you and Mum in us all. It's a pretty amazing legacy.

I know you worked hard, and you and Mum gave us the most important things to sustain us, and for that I'll be forever grateful.

You were very short on advice, I guess because you wanted us to find our own way, but there is one piece of advice I think your generation had wrong. You said on the day I got back from Vietnam that I should forget and just get on with my life. But I couldn't ever forget that I went. I couldn't push aside the memories of the mates who died, and I could never stop being a mate to those who survived and continued to struggle through their own lives. I'm pretty sure, in hindsight, that you would have carried on the same way.

You were a much-loved person to your family, your network of friends and your workmates. Your gregarious nature was endowed upon us kids, and your generous nature passed on to us all. This generosity of spirit is still being carried in the everyday lives of your spawn.

You always said, 'I came into the world naked. If I go out the same way, at least I broke even.' Well, judging by the number of friends who came to your funeral to bid you farewell, your profit was the spirit, memories and smiles you left behind.

I wish life was different, and that I was able to say these things in person, but you left us so suddenly we were bereft of words.

Love,

Normie

Normie Rowe AM: the original King of Pop

Caro Papa

I want to tell you that I love you. I am so grateful for everything you taught me and for the times we had together. I wish you could be around to see your grandkids, you would be so proud.

I'm sad I couldn't be there at the end, but maybe it was for the best because by all accounts the cancer was pretty bad. I know you knew you were sick for a long time, but you didn't tell anyone or go to the doctor. I think you were scared of what they might find, so you let it go too long.

I'll never forget seeing you in that hospital bed; it's the only time I've ever seen fear in your eyes. You looked so weak and drained it broke my heart, but I covered it well because I wanted to be strong for you.

You were such a formidable man: five times Italian champion kayaker; Olympian at the 1952 Helsinki games; you spoke seven languages; you had a photographic memory, you could recite all the classics. The king of the Tiber reduced to being bedridden and helpless. As I left the hospital I knew in my heart that you'd be gone soon.

Like most men of your generation, you never spoke about your feelings. It must have been hard raising seven brothers and two sisters when you yourself were only sixteen. You had to grow up too soon, my dearest Dad.

Not having you around during my childhood in Australia was tough and without any positive role models I lost my way in my teens. I got pretty wild. Whenever I would go back to see you or you would come out here, we would clash. I think I was angry at you for not being around regularly and resented the attempt to parent me for one month of the year. It must have been hard for you too – I was pretty angry.

I had self-esteem issues for most of my life but I am good now, Dad. I've been clean for ten years and realise that the only person I need to be okay with is me. I have found peace in my life and I have a family who loves me. Life is good.

I have tried to be a good father, but man it's a tough gig sometimes! It has helped me understand you and Mum better, though. If I could rewrite the last two decades I would only ask for one thing, the one thing you couldn't give me: more time with you.

I miss you, Dad, and every memory of you fills me with sadness and love all at once. Until we next meet, rest in peace, Papa.

Love always, your son,

Steve

Steve Bastoni: actor, founder of the Peninsula Film Festival

Dear Dad

Thanks for letting me into your shed. Even though I mostly just sat in one 'safe' spot and watched, I still learned a lot. I actually think you liked the company, at least until the 'Off you go, get out of here and go play somewhere else.'

'Zrrooomph zrrooomph' was the soundtrack of my childhood, the sound of timber going through the thicknesser. Every time I peered into your shed you always had your head over the big green lathe machine, turning yet *another* leg of *another* table. You turned that timber until it looked like a dancer in the middle of an impossible pirouette; it was a privilege to see you at your self-taught best (except that time when you made a sideboard that was too big to get out of the shed!)

Maybe I take after you, because I can use all types of power tools now. I haven't told you that I can use a drop saw; I know you'll just worry. Perhaps that's the reason why you never took me under your wing in the shed. I'm fairly sure it wasn't because I was a girl … maybe more because if I ever got hurt you would never forgive yourself.

I will always inhale the smell of freshly sawn wood and think of you, Dad, and those days in the shed. I hope that's okay with you.

Love,

Amber Joy

Amber Joy Poulton: country music sensation

Dear Dad

Mum once told me, 'When you were born, your father wasn't allowed to see you for three days.' That's because in Yugoslavia, as it was then, and at that time, the rule was that fathers couldn't visit newborns for three days. But you insisted. You said, 'My daughter's been born – I want to go in and see her. I don't want to wait any more!' You've never been shy about saying what you want. And they let you in.

'When your father held you,' Mum told me, 'I saw a golden light shoot through and around your dad, and around you. I know this sounds crazy, but I saw it. It was an experience that nobody would believe unless they were there.'

The light that connected you and me has bound us together always. You always were, and still are, a very strong, confident protector. You've been strict – I learnt how to cook and clean and look after a vegetable garden at a much younger age than anyone else I know! But you also have the biggest heart of gold.

I've had ups in my life as well as plenty of downs – you've been there for all of it. I know that I wouldn't be who I am without you – and maybe you wouldn't be who you are without me. After all, you tell me that I'm your favourite child …

Love,

Jackie

Jackie Gillies: businesswoman, psychic medium turned Real Housewife of Melbourne

Dear Dad

You're a man of few words, so I'll take a leaf from your book …
You're my hero. Always were, always will be.

Love you to the moon and back × infinity.

Ben

Ben Gillies: Silverchair legend

Dear Dad

I don't know if I ever told you that I was always very proud of you. You were an honest, hard-working and respected man in our town. You and Ned Doyle were the main fathers who did what you could to improve the grounds of our little school. As a farmer, it was you who the CSIRO chose to plant and trial new varieties of wheat.

When you arrived home after ten hours on the tractor cultivating our land, the family's eyes lit up with pride as you took off your hat to reveal a white forehead. The rest of your face was red with Mallee dust. Your good set of teeth shone like diamonds.

We knew you were also proud of us.

You weren't only a farmer; the local band relied on your rhythm banjo to keep the tempo tight on the dancefloor. The whole district was also proud of your pure tenor voice, and you and Mum delighted everybody with duets.

You belted my bottom with your rough, old hands a couple of times, but you always seemed to regret it. I think it was

Mum's idea, if I was particularly naughty. Your words are clear in my ears still: you didn't ever want your boys to be afraid of you, as you were of your dad. And we weren't. In fact, I thought sometimes you were too soft for not standing up to our very strong mother.

I also enjoyed your love of cars, especially V8s. You had a heavy foot but we always felt 100 per cent safe. Mum was happy to sleep as we reached 80 mph on the highways. My love of cars comes from that, I'm sure, and my lead foot. However, I'm a mug mechanic compared to you. That skill went to one of your other sons, Pete.

Well, Dad, you were never a good listener and a little bit too God-fearing for me, but I could not have wished for a better dad.

John

John Williamson AM: 'True Blue' Aussie icon

Dear Dad

When I saw you standing in the doorway of my grandmother's house, six-foot-tall in dark jeans, blue RM Williams shirt and high-heeled riding boots, topped off with a ten-gallon hat and a Luger pistol hanging low off your hip, I did not know that you would be my dad.

Lucky for five-year-old me, you fell in love with my mother that day. You took Mum, me and my younger brother and sister to your cattle station to be part of your dream to be the Cattle King of the Northern Territory.

The dream grew rapidly: four cattle stations, the best cattle and horses, helicopters, Mercedes-Benz cars and seven more children. We were the Ten Tapp Kids.

Along with this came the stresses of life for you and Mum. Lots of people to care for led to lots of sleepless nights. Mogadon, Valium and Johnnie Walker Black Label became your best friends.

My final vision of you: standing on the steps of the Supreme Court in Darwin as the family fought off the receivers and banks. You were broken and sad, and I didn't know what to say or how to help. You were to die at your beloved Killarney Station just a few months later.

I wish I had asked you if you were okay. We are not good at showing love in our family, but I think you knew I loved you, and I know you loved me.

Love,

Toni

Toni Tapp Coutts: author and former cattle wrangler

Dear Dad

I am writing this letter to someone I don't really know – you, my dad. Because you died when I was only five.

I don't have a memory of your face, your voice, your temperament … my only memory of you is sitting on your lap and rubbing my little fingers up against your whiskers.

You must have been a good dad because my brother and two sisters turned out to be great people, and even though Mum battled through the war years to bring us up, with rationing, an outside dunny, one bathroom and no shower, I never felt we were poor because our house was so warm and full of music. So you must have married the right woman.

I'm sure you'll be glad to know the loss of you didn't harm or handicap me. I just would have liked to have known you, that's all.

While writing this letter I have now imagined you giving the speech at my:

21st birthday (you would have been 81)

wedding (you would have been 91)

1st child's birth (you would have been – ouch! – 123)

I have never before imagined those scary figures – because you were never part of my consciousness … until now.

As I write this letter, after 79 years, I realise what I might have missed.

Your son,

Alan

Alan 'Hoppy' Hopgood AM: playwright, actor, icon

Dear Dad

I'm glad. I'm glad about a lot of things.

Glad you made up lots of words so that I didn't know the difference between them and the ones that get used by normal people, leading to some mildly embarrassing (but, looking back, endearing) moments.

Glad that we have a silly song for any occasion, such as 'the dog doing laps around the house' or the 'going to the toilet before bed' song.

Glad that you taught me how to listen to the country around me.

Glad you made up that game 'Hockelo' on the horses in the red dust of the drought.

Glad I inherited your knack and love of arguing for the sake of it; that's a bit of fun, hey family?!

Glad you yarned around the campfire growing up, so I could learn to yarn in the form of songs to strangers all over the country and call it work.

Glad you are getting all the joy out of being a top-notch papa to our little Walby-bear (aka Walter aka your grandson – but you already know that).

Glad we taught you that crying is cool (and helpful) and that sharing your feelings is liberating.

Glad you gave me my super sibs and that we all inherited your extremely thick hair.

Mostly, glad that you're my dad.

And don't worry, I won't ever forget the bush.

Huzz nuzz buzz fuzz

Fanny Lumsden: muso, founder of Red Dirt Road Records

Dear Dad

My big, tall, moustache-wearing papa, this is our 22nd year on borrowed time. It's 22 years since you were bitten by a junkie on the arm, 22 years since, because of said bite, you had tests that told us you had a silent cancer growing inside you that would have taken you from us within twelve months.

How can this person who bit you be walking around, not knowing the difference they made in our lives? They don't know that, because of them, you were at my 21st birthday and we danced together to 'A Little Ray of Sunshine', or that you were at my wedding, where we danced to 'The Way You Look Tonight', or that we went on a trip to London together, or that you were there for the big moments in my career that wouldn't have meant as much had you not been there. They don't know that because of them, you are a grandfather. Because of them you saw parts of the world you wouldn't have. Because of them we have shared in your love of music for longer. Because of them Mum still has you by her side, as you both turn 70. Because of them an abundance of people who love you, were spared having to say goodbye too soon. Because of them Collingwood has had the most passionate (crazy) supporter for another 22 years. Because of them we can argue our political views. Because of them we have our dad, husband, pa, uncle, brother, cousin, friend, golf buddy, justice of the peace.

They will never know that because of them, our lives are better, and we have no way to thank them.

But I know. And I think about it all the time. And I thank them. With all my heart.

Christie x

Christie Whelan Browne: stage and television actor

Dear Dad

This is the first and only letter I have written to you; so many things to say, it's hard to know exactly where to begin.

July 1950 was a hard year for Mum, the two nanas and the two pops, as that was the month and year that you passed away – due to the illnesses you contracted while a prisoner of war. I was only two years old, however I do have a foggy, blurred memory of you with a bandaged leg. When I mentioned this to my mother years later, she was surprised that I could remember.

You wouldn't recognise the world you left. So much has changed: men on the moon; another two wars; television (that's movies at home); a telephone you carry with you – and it can also send photographs; an electrical device called a computer that allows you to access information 24 hours a day. So many changes ... in fact, too many to mention. It might even feel like an alien world to you.

But the most important thing: even though you are gone, you are not, as your genes and your very being lives on in me, your three grandchildren and your two great-grandchildren.

Unfortunately your era wasn't one in which a lot of photographs were taken – or was that just our family? However, in the ones that I do have, you echo in all of us. I see glimpses of you all the time, in each of us.

You wouldn't believe this but a number of years ago someone passed a letter on to me. Lo and behold it was from Bill Young. Yes – the same Bill you were a prisoner of war with; you were both recaptured after escaping from Sandakan. So of course I went to see him. What a beautiful man! And Dad, did he have some lovely things to say about you. He filled in a lot of blanks for me (obviously, when you got back you didn't talk to Mum about your experiences – too painful). He told me you and your mates protected him from beatings by the guards, sometimes copping the hidings instead of him, all because he was much younger than the rest of you. By the way, Bill is over 90 now – still going strong, and a wonderful man.

Your grandchildren and I often talk and think about you; in fact, your grandson has a tattoo of you on his thigh – taken from one of your old army photos. It's a great likeness.

Age shall not weary them – to all of us, you'll always be that young soldier with the beautiful smile. But to me you'll always be Dad.

Love,

Russell

Russell Morris AM: singer/songwriter ('The Real Thing')

Dear Dad

So, I'm buying a suit and the guy says, 'We can put a little tab at the waist so you don't need to wear a belt.' The only thing I could think at that moment was the excellent trick you passed on to me: if you're in a meeting and you think your fly might be down, pretend you're adjusting your belt and with your middle finger check if you can feel the zipper at the top! It's a brilliant life hack.

Anyway, anyway, I'm at the suit shop because, guess what? I'm getting married! Sorry, probably should have led with that. You would love her, really. She's kind, funny, smart, generous and very good-looking. You absolutely would have flirted with her. She, as my girlfriends past did, would have fallen for your charm and hoped to heck that I ended up like you.

We're eloping – it's cool, you're not missing anything. I'm missing you, of course, but don't worry, I'm not wrecked like I was, and now when I think about you I can smile. Your humour, keen brain, the way you would always give advice to everyone, your ridiculously huge laugh, your unconditional love. I see you in my brother, his son, in me. I do wish you'd met my girl, though.

Anyway, I decided not to get the pants tab. I mean, how would you be able to check your fly? I miss you, mate. Come watch the wedding, eh?

Toby x

Toby Truslove: comedic actor and long-time adorer of Wendy James from Transvision Vamp

Dear Dad

I still now go to call you to talk about my day, and I sometimes do, but your phone has since been disconnected so I can no longer hear your voice.

You were what I consider a cheeky dad. You didn't comply with the norm of what a dad should be, but you were still mine.

I want to say thank you. I don't know if I ever thanked you for getting up at 1 am six days a week for three years to drive me to work during my apprenticeship, and then make the 45-minute trip home again before getting back up yet again at 7 am to start work.

I feel like I owe it to you to be the best I can in my career, as you sacrificed your time to ensure I had a great start. I hope I have made you proud.

I want to thank you for your love of all things potatoes that I have continued on with my family, making it a family staple and the sixth official food group.

I sometimes wonder if you are looking down on me, watching, and as I scramble through life I think about how you would direct me if you were still here.

You didn't want to let cancer win. As long as you were still working you felt like you were beating it and showing it who was boss. You worked up till the day before you passed, and you fought so hard for six years.

I miss you.

Kirsten

Kirsten Tibballs: much-loved pastry chef and MasterChef Australia's 'Queen of Chocolate'

Dear Dad

BLONDIE

My father's lost outside,
Searching down and outback streets in Sydney, for his pride.
It's left him now, doesn't matter where, when or how,
He won't take a hero's bow.
They look into the world expecting heroes,
To save them from their normal, lifeless lives,
They don't understand, the world is filled with heroes
Working hard just to survive.

That's part of a song I wrote for you, the 'other' Kevin Bennett. You disappeared from our lives when I was eighteen, just didn't come home one day, which was compounded by the fact that Mum had already left.

Everyone was convinced you'd done a runner from Sydney where you never belonged, back to your country roots, but I was to find out the truth in a brutally unbelievable way. A friend and I were heading up Elizabeth Street in 1978 (I was

26) to cruise the famous Goulburn Street second-hand record shops, when I caught a glimpse of this old, obviously homeless man with long, grey hair shuffling by. I mentioned that it looked like my father, and my mate laughed and said, 'As if.'

I had to agree, but I needed to know, so I turned and followed him. When I got close, I called out his nickname, 'Blondie', and sure enough, he turned around. It was him and he didn't have a clue who I was – he asked if I might be one of the McGlashan boys from Baradine. I told him that my name was the same as his. His reply: 'Ya got twenty bucks?'

Dear Dad, Blondie, finally I understand ... Happy Father's Day.

Kevin

Kevin Bennett: ARIA nominated singer/songwriter

Dear ...

Well, that's the issue, isn't it? It comes down to a matter of terminology in the absence of anything else. *Father* works, with its biological connotations, but the word, somewhat unavoidably, also drags a whole slew of familial baggage in its wake, and simply won't do. There's so little here that it's important to ensure everything is correct.

Dad, needless to say, is right out. *Progenitor* is accurate. At least, I think so, although I'm pretty sure you'd disagree. I remember that vile email reply your wife sent me – three years ago, after I finally gave up any hope of ever meeting you, then got on the front foot, and wrote to you one final time.

'*We always knew you weren't his; he only took you in out of kindness.*' Except she didn't use a semi-colon. And I'm not sure you ever took me in. If you did, perhaps I would have some memory of you, rather than just the understanding (spoken about quietly and rarely, I assume, by my mother talking to her mother, overheard by the little boy in the next room) that

I was about eighteen months old when she took me from the military camp in Malaysia, where you remained.

I often wondered about you: who you were, where you were, and whether you missed me. Somewhere in my mid-30s I decided to track you down, using your name, rank and serial number, written on my birth certificate. It took a while, but eventually you responded.

For the next twenty years I tried to spark up a written conversation that was more than desultory, even holding out the vague hope that one day perhaps you might like to visit your firstborn, so I could meet you. Never happened, did it? Never mind. I'm actually writing this to thank you. I have my own son now, and already he's been in my company six times longer than I was ever in yours. He has no grandfather, as I have no father, but we have each other and always will have – secure in the knowledge that I am not, and perhaps never have been, you.

Andrew

Andrew Masterson: author, journalist and editor of Cosmos

Dear Dad

I think the next time I come home we should record another interview. The first interview runs over four hours, and yet we only got to when you were 27. About to leave the Grenadier Guards in England and hitchhike around the world – that's where we got to.

I know what comes next: India, Pakistan, Singapore; but there's something special about having a recording. It complements the photographs. This process makes me wonder what my generation is going to pore over when we're old. We don't print photographs any more. So, what then? 'Gather round children and let me tell you about these permalinks'?

There was the home video that made it into our family lore. We'd been on holiday, and everyone was sitting around the television, watching. Onscreen, you narrated something about the scenery, and then you let the camera fall to your side. You thought it was off. Then you recorded yourself crunching over some gravel – straight into the men's toilets. We screamed. Where did that VCR go?

And these audio clips. They're recorded on my iPhone, which I've been told is how most journalists now record their interviews anyway. But I'm no digital archivist. When we were packing up my apartment I found a cassette. I don't know what's on it, and until I get a player I can't find out. Maybe Grandad's voice is trapped in there, singing in the kitchen as Nanny makes butter toast.

Anyway. Maybe you have some ideas.

Charlotte

Charlotte Guest: poet

Dear Dad

I've had a lot of time, in this life, to think about fathers. And mothers. About nature versus nurture. That tends to happen when you grow up with parents who aren't biologically related to you but you wish they were. Being adopted has never been a problem, though, and that's as much to do with you as it is with Mum. I always was, and am still, your 'favourite daughter' – your only daughter.

You couldn't have been more excited to take me home from hospital, and I still remember you saying that you could have taken all those babies home. But it was me you carried away to Gordon Street, me and my brother you buried in sand up to our necks on the beach and taught to bodysurf, and for whom you drew elaborate Easter-egg-treasure-hunt maps. Me whose ankle got ruined in the wheel of your bicycle because, well, dads can't be perfect all the time. Now the scar that's left tells me a story about when I was so little I could sit in front of you on the seat.

By the time 'bio dad', as I called him, died in 2012, we had not met – because I hadn't wanted to. One father was all I ever needed and one father was all I ever had. That one was you, and I have been so lucky.

Love,

Sophie

Sophie Green: author and publisher

Dear Dad

I'd like to take back the Father's Day gift you received in 1968.

I was born on Father's Day in 1968. It appeared I was your Father's Day present. I wasn't. You did not deserve me. You did not deserve any of us. You were not a good man. You were not a good father. It was deeply unfair you were given so much and we had so much taken away.

You died a few years ago. I don't know what year, nor do I know the date. I was working when I received my sister's text: 'The cunt's dead.' I simply glanced at it and continued to address the class I was running. I felt happy, relieved, liberated, at peace.

You were a horrible man. A messer. A narcissist. I am glad you're dead. I never let you meet my kids because you were not worthy of them. I didn't go to your funeral. Every Father's Day without you is a celebration for me. It's been decades since I liberated myself from you and the myth of the father I should have had. Father's Day is hard and complicated for many people. And on that day those people are in my thoughts.

Every day I pay tribute to the amazing parents I see around me. Parents who are doing their very best despite being poorly parented themselves or having challenging children. I cheer for the children who are doing incredible things and living amazing lives despite being poorly parented by horrible people.

Someone said to me yesterday, 'Your boys are great. You've done a great job.' I said, 'I take no credit. They are who they are. They got lucky to be born who they are.'

She tried to argue with me a little. I said, 'You and I both know amazing parents with horrible kids and horrible parents with amazing kids. I decided to have children. I live up to my own idea of what that commitment and responsibility is. How they turn out, they turn out. I just need to know I have done my best. Lived up to my standards. The rest is up to them.' Who or what your children are is no reflection on who you are.

Clinging to the idea of the perfect Disney father is damaging. For everyone. But particularly for those people who experienced abusive relationships. Trying to round an abusive or dysfunctional relationship up to normal creates cognitive dissonance, damage and sets a terrible example of what love is, what relationships are and what 'normal' looks like.

I raise a glass to all the humans out there doing their best. I see you and I thank you. You are making a difference to people who are not even born yet. How do I know that? Because I was born. I was born on Father's Day.

But it was also my birthday. I choose to celebrate that. Love conquers all x

Catherine

Catherine Deveny: risk-taker, untamed brumby, mainstream media pariah

Dear Dad

You've been gone seventeen years now. In recent weeks, while doing a long-overdue clean-up at home, I came across some of your documents. In the months after you died, I'd sorted through your clutter, which, I think it's fair to say, made mine look like a molehill against your mountain. But I overlooked several exercise books.

What a find! I discovered poems of yours that I had never seen before. Written in your meticulous Yiddish hand. One exercise book is headed: *Songs Written in the Early Youthful Years*. It contains perhaps the very first poem you wrote. Titled, 'A Shepherd'.

You were twenty at the time, living in the Polish city of Bialystok. You wrote: *How good it is to be a shepherd / how good it is to be present / as the sun makes its way east to west / and pours into the mouth of the world / so many buckets full of warm glow.* Towards the end of the poem, you see yourself drinking *the fresh dew, and moisture from the swamps, through my bare feet.* I can relate to that.

You retired at 70, in distant Melbourne. After a detour of four decades, working in factories and at your Victoria Markets stall, you returned to your first love, writing Yiddish poetry. The final sixteen years of your life, from 70 till your death at 86, were your best and most creative.

Towards the end you were a wiry gnome, trotting through the streets of North Carlton, spending time in the neighbourhood park, relishing every moment. Returning to your backyard vegetable patch, and to the makeshift desk, the dressing table in the front room, and to your beloved poets.

After your death in 1992, I found the draft of your final poem, written that very morning. Some lines are crossed out, others rewritten. It includes the line, *I feel like a little leaf about to fall into the universe.*

What a way to go. Your work is done. The shepherd can rest.

I am approaching those years now. The circle is closing. You have paved the way. And I walk it with bare feet.

Hugs,

Arnold

Arnold Zable: acclaimed writer, novelist, storyteller and human rights advocate

Dear Dad

When my body was smaller than I remember, you took me into the sea and let the water wash over me. With my pale body in your arms, you waded out through the shallows. Sand shifting underneath, you moved slowly. Like pink light fading. Like darkness descending. You lowered me into blue.

The sea enveloped me the way night envelops day. Everything was changed. Because from that moment on, my life would resemble the shape of water.

Later, I'd paddle beyond the break, and you'd teach me how to read the swells as they climbed out of the deep. With you, a wall of water would open like a book, long sentences written in curls of turquoise. And suddenly, it wouldn't matter what my life would turn into onshore, back behind the trees, because I'd found a home here, under the horizon. A place where I could breathe.

Later, you'd take me out on a wooden yacht you'd helped design, and you'd teach me how to read wind. You'd point to dark patches of water, and you'd say, *see*, look how it moves.

And we'd watch together as the patches of darkness fanned out across the bay. Into nothing. Into everything. *See*, it's coming closer, you'd whisper. And then it would be upon us, and I'd feel the wind brush up against me, rising up, filling the sails so that they spread out wide like skin around bone.

Later, you'd tell me that sailing is about listening. You'd say, the ocean sings to the yacht, and the yacht sings back. Then you'd smile, and you'd say, sailing is about being quiet, listening to that song and adjusting yourself accordingly.

Because it's all about surrender, not force.

Later, I'd be in the library at Oxford, where I'm studying, and in the middle of reading a passage about the ocean's multiplicity, a message would pop up from you saying you miss me. And I'd think about how even though tides move in opposite directions, they're part of the same body. Multiple parts, making one whole.

I'd picture you, on the other side of the world, all the oceans between us, and I'd think, *Thank you, Dad. Thank you for teaching me the language of the sea.*

Love,

Floss

Sophie Hardcastle: Provost's Scholar, author, artist, screenwriter

Dear Dad

I want to show my appreciation for being awesome. Here's a list of things (you know I love a good list, like you) that pop into my mind and they all start with *Thanks* ...

For smiling every day and whistling and singing while you work. For teaching me how to bait a hook and cast a line. For hugs on the couch by the fire in winter and stories on the trampoline under the stars in summer. For growing spinach, cucumbers, mulberries, watermelon, peas, carrots, grapes and everything else in your garden that you let me help myself to.

For paying for piano lessons that turned into singing and guitar lessons. For driving us to the beach every Christmas holidays towing the caravan. For being born in Tamworth and staying in your hometown. For your practical fix-it solutions to problems, and showing me the value of commonsense. For loving music and taking us to concerts of touring acts outside of festival time. For your old-fashioned manners, like, 'Men walk curb side, please.' For playing country records, radio and cassettes really loudly and letting us sing along, especially in the car on long trips in the yellow Valiant. For letting us rearrange the lounge room for ABBA concerts. For teaching me how to make damper in the camp oven and to love the sound of nature at night.

For showing me how to change a tyre, check the oil and anything 'yellow' under the hood. For the lesson in 'don't take what's not yours' when I took your coin collection for my own piggy bank. For good advice about buying a car ... oh, and how to drive one. For knowing when it was a 'Mum' problem to solve. For stern words when I broke the light on the outside of the house with the tennis ball when you had asked me many times to stop. For letting me earn $100 pocket money in the workshop so I could buy my first guitar ... I still live by the rule, 'Don't buy what you can't afford.'

For letting me go. For letting me come back. For letting me make mistakes and not roasting me for it. For covering my favourite *chaise longue* that I sit on every day, which makes me happy.

For being a kind man who taught me how to say hello to a stranger, give people a chance, listen to others and be forgiving.

For many other amazing experiences, guidance and opportunities I will have for a lifetime.

You're the best dad a daughter could ever want.

I LOVE YOU, don't forget it.

Fliss xx

Felicity Urquhart: multi-award winning songstress

Hey Dad_____ ,

I cherish everything you've done for me, including... how you pinned my ankles together when I was a baby and left me to perish on a mountain. And how, years later, you tried to run me off the road at an intersection, then whacked me on the head with a stick.

Sorry that... you died.

I should have... not killed you.

On the upside... when it came to light that you were my dad, our wife hanged herself, and I poked out my own eyes.

I'm grateful that our paths crossed because as a result I learned that... I had the capacity to father children who were also my siblings.

If things had unfolded differently for us, then I would never have been blessed with the wonderful opportunity to... develop a serious complex and to fill out this bullshit closure exercise in this bullshit Gratitude Journal.

Be well,

Oedipus
_____

(Translated by Julie Koh: Short-story writer)

Dear Dad

Because of you, I was always the coolest kid at school. My friends had dads who took them to see *Star Wars*. My dad was in it. My friends had dads who rented *Flash Gordon* on VCR from Blockbusters. My dad was in it. My friends had dads who enjoyed light-on-fizz lemon soft drinks – my dad was the Solo Man. Like, the actual Solo Man. Incidentally, that titbit of information has also made me the coolest kid with some ever-so-slightly older ladies in my life. The very memory of the Solo Man still solicits a faint knee-tremble I'm sure you'd be proud to know.

But it's not just your impressive CV that makes me so proud to be your son. Your work ethic is second-to-none, your ability to create something out of nothing is genius, your complete devotion to your family and friends is glorious … plus your fabulous wardrobe would be truly enviable to anybody. There aren't many straight men who can rock a single pearl necklace, but you do. There aren't many comedians who could avoid an obvious pearl necklace joke, but I do. Coz I'm classy. Like my dad.

Thank you for never judging me, who I am and what I want to do. I know you probably would have liked a son who played football on the weekends rather than my own one-man renditions of *The Phantom of the Opera* in its entirety (complete with costumes of course), but you never once stopped me from chasing my dream. Instead, you have been a constant pillar of support, friendship, love and advice. You have been there at every step, and literally every show. Every high and every low (this is sounding a bit like a Celine Dion song now, but you get my drift).

I love watching you in a crowd. You're the life of any party and have a magical way of making every person you meet feel special and important. I love how you treat women with utter equality, respect and class, most especially my sisters Holly and Alice and my spectacular mum, Jenny. I love that you worship Mum just as I do. You've shown me how to make a marriage work and it's inspiring. I truly think the world is lacking more fabulous men like you.

I'm in actual awe of how hard you've worked to give our family a spectacular life.

The best word to describe you really would be fabulous. You are *fabulous!* But I think you already know that.

And thank you for allowing me to be fabulous. As fucking fabulous as I want to be.

I love you, Dad.

Joel

Joel Creasey: stand-up comedian, actor and television presenter

Dear Dad

Thirty-five years ago I came out to you late one night in our living room. It was one of the hardest things I have ever done. I was sure you did not want your daughter to be a lesbian. And I desperately did not want to disappoint you.

What a horrible situation it was for us both. But the truth had been chipping away at me. I hated lying to you and everyone else.

While I knew that what I was was okay (homosexuality had been decriminalised in South Australia nine years earlier), the fact remained that this was the early 1980s, and I doubt there were many fathers on Planet Earth who hoped their child would one day say, 'Hey Dad, I'm gay.' So the best I thought I could expect was tolerance.

You gave me that.

As the years progressed you even started to embrace my girlfriends. I could see you were really trying. I was so grateful. Not because I should be grateful for being accepted for who I am, but because I knew you had to overcome something big in yourself. I knew it didn't come easily and I knew how much you must have loved me to do this.

Last year Australia was voting on whether to allow gay people to marry. Mum sent me a photo of 78-year-old you, walking your Jack Russell, Max, whose coat was emblazoned with the words *I Support Same Sex Marriage*.

I have rarely cried as I cried when I saw that picture, as I cry writing this to you now. You will never know how much your love means to me.

Your daughter,

Johanna

Joh Jarvis: journalist and former ABC media executive

Dear Dad

Well I know I've killed you off a bunch of times in a number of songs I've written over the years, but I am sincerely stoked that you're still alive!

I now know it's not easy being a dad – especially to teenagers – but what overrides the hurts and frustrations of the past is knowing, to my absolute core, that I am loved. Your ongoing support, loyalty and dependability with me, Mum and our whole family is true 'love in action'. Words schmurds! Nothing says 'I love you' like servitude.

Even 50 years into it – when I asked if you felt like getting arrested with me – you replied 'Sure', even before knowing what the hell I was on about. But then to witness you once again walk your talk and be able to spend the day together in your old backyard – on the once-mighty Namoi River near Boggabri – where we 'locked on' to that fucking corrupt, immoral, giant water pump (belonging to the heart- and life-breaking Maules Creek coal mine), before being cut off and loaded into the back of a paddy wagon (where you asked the sergeant where the beer fridge was!) – and then to spend the rest of the day locked up in a police cell ... well, for me that was one of the greatest days ever, and I shall remember it way beyond this life.

Thanks for the lessons on how and what it means to love. You're an inspiration, old fella, and I wish you (and Mum) all the greatest – always.

Happy Father's Day, mate.

Luke

Luke O'Shea: country music star

Dear Dad

Happy Father's Day! I'm thinking you probably won't read this, but if you do it'll be while you're on the toilet, for hours, contemplating life while also pondering the consistently reliable *NT News*.

First of all I know that we have not gotten on particularly well over the years, but the fact that you're a stanch hothead German and I'm an Aboriginal gay drag queen … well, just to be in the same room together for more than one hour really makes me happy and gives me hope for a better future in life generally.

Dad, I'll never forget the embedded memories in my head, like the day you wanted to teach me to bowl and I tried to run away and you tripped me and broke my arm in two places then stated, 'It's okay', as you tried to bend it back into place, making it much worse than it was. Or the time you took me fishing and as a joke thought it would be funny to throw me over the side of the dinghy. Or the many, many times you'd chase me with frogs, snakes and lizards as a hilarious joke.

Although these memories have scarred me for life in a deep, $150-per-hour regular-psychiatrist-session way, it will be the other memories that live in my heart, the ones that have forever changed me and which make me smile.

Thank you, Dad, for your unwavering passion for the things you love in life and for what you stand for and believe in. Thank you for your generosity, heart, humour and love for humanity.

Thank you for accepting me as an openly gay (fabulously sassy) man and allowing me to live my truth.

I love you, Dad, and hope you know, see and believe that.

Love your son,

Ben x

(aka Miss Ellaneous)
Ben Graetz: drag queen extraordinaire

Dear Dad

Dear Bern
Dear Dad
I kissed you on the cold forehead,
a moment, a sensation that I cannot forget.
I didn't want to,
I wanted to,
I didn't want to.

But more –
I didn't want to have any regret.
I didn't think that I would have more regret kissing a
    cold forehead
than the regret I'd feel if I'd opted out.

My lips on your cold, yellow forehead:
it repulsed me.
I have lost the sensation now – it's a memory,
but for the first two, maybe three years, I could feel the

sensation of your cold forehead on the skin of my lips
and it made me feel
sick.

When we were little
you were the best dad anyone could wish for;
you fired imaginations,
stoked silly senses of humour,
and ignited passions for stories.
You showed me how to love country and how to explore
and how to love dogs.

But it's a bugger the booze got you –
you left, and the addict replaced you;
such a pity,
the supremely unconventional, irreverent, romantic and
    unshakeably honest man
left
and was replaced
by a shadow
without guts,
hollowed
and
untruthful.

What a pity.

The play was still there in this shadow
as you talked about how you could still fly a plane (if only
    they'd let you out)

and spoke of the 'ode' you'd just written to my mother,
the word 'ode' delivered with your characteristic, playful
    flourish –
a magic twinkle in your saffron-yellow eye
as your jaundicing skin peeled,
your over-taxed organs failed,
and you complained about the home
and asked for more wine.

What a pity this got you;
you could have lived for a long time,
with the constitution of an ox,
but this got you, Dad – Bern –
what a pity.

Even oxen can take a beating
and lose.

What a pity.

Penelope

*Penelope Bartlau: performance creator, puppeteer and director for
the Women's Circus*

Dear Dad

I followed you, I ran to you; you held me and still do.

I am your baby girl who followed you everywhere. Anything you worked on, I was your trades-girl passing the nails to you.

Picnics, swimming and soccer, that was our thing. I had no fear when you were there. You provided a home and food on our table each and every day.

You love the simple things in life. Just being with us all, the family, is number one for you.

I used to think I looked like you, but I am adopted and Aboriginal and not blood to you, but I was and still am my dad's little girl.

When the school was accusing me of things I didn't do, there you were sorting them out. When I got my first job and they falsely accused me of stealing, there you were standing up for me. When I was sad about people looking at me or staring in an odd way, you would say, 'That's 'cause you're beautiful.' You never pointed at my nationality as being an oddity; beauty was all that you saw in me.

Where did I go wrong and stop seeing myself as you see me? I swapped beauty for trauma. Still, you never gave up on me in those traumatic years. I can see it now, the beauty within me; that's because of you.

Love means you, and you mean love to me.

Shellie

Shellie Morris: proud Yanyuwa and Wardaman woman, singer, ambassador for Adopt Change

Dear Dad

You know that cliché about how changing a baby's nappy doesn't smell when it's your own child? Well, my kids must be the milkman's, because damn it stinks! It wasn't until I had to change their nappies that I realised just how much you did for me, and how much shit you had to put up with, as a father. I suppose that's a cliché in itself, but at least it's true. So, thank you. And, sorry.

Thank you for all those nights when you had to hold your hand on my chest and rock me to sleep, because if you didn't I'd sit up and ask for more food. Thank you for carrying me from the car to bed when I was pretending to be asleep, even though you had a bad back from carrying me to bed so many times.

Thank you for reading to me every single night and passing on your love of books. Thank you for letting me eat bread dipped in cream and honey while you did, because that's what they ate in *The Hobbit*.

Thank you for the little lessons, like teaching me how to

cook two-minute noodles (the secret is to boil them for three minutes). Another lesson: don't believe in scumbag advertising.

Thank you for the big lessons, like the value of hard work, being kind to others, being honest, being loyal, and teaching me how to drive a car because Mum was too scared. Sorry for doing a U-turn right in front of another car and almost getting your precious Commodore wagon T-boned to the shithouse.

Sorry also for my ingratitude and ratbaggery as a kid. Sorry for projectile vomiting on the back of your neck after getting carsick in primary school. Sorry for projectile vomiting in the car after you picked me up drunk from a party in high school. Sorry for stealing your beers out of the fridge before said party.

Sorry for making you wait in the cold and dark at the beach because I just needed to catch 'one more wave'. Sorry for ignoring a lot of your good advice. Don't worry, I'm going to pass it onto my kids one day so they can ignore it as well.

I'll end now with another cliché. The apple doesn't fall far from the tree. I'm so proud that I'm so similar to you, but love that you're most proud of all the ways I'm different. Because of my boys, who are the apple of my eye, I finally know how much you've loved me all these years.

Why there are so many apples in parenting clichés I'm not sure, but now I'm hungry. 'Nice to meet you, Hungry, I'm Dad,' I hear you say. Something I now say daily myself, followed by, 'Have an apple.' Cheers for that one too.

Tim (aka Hungry)

Tim Hawken: author and journalist

Dear Dad

Thought you'd like to know I have a box of your photographic negatives. I've had them for many years now – the box with all the white envelopes. About 150 negatives: weddings, portraits, servicemen going to war, mums and babies ... The earliest one is dated 1946.

I look at them and feel your presence. I can hear you say, 'Look at that! Are you looking? Look closely!' It's like you're right next to me, whispering in my ear.

The smell of the film brings you into the room with me, Dad. I look through them now and reminisce about the many, many hours we spent together looking at these same photos when I was twelve, thirteen, fourteen years old.

Remember how you would tell me a story about each one? Who was in it, where you were, pointing out tiny details I didn't notice; you *made* me look. You told me you liked to find out about people, always wanted to make them feel good before you snapped their picture.

A few years later you told me to try to find work you love and that makes the people around you feel better about themselves. In return, you feel better about yourself and maybe get a great photo!

I'll be looking through them again today, Dad, still feeling you here.

Love you, Pops, from your son,

Allen

Allen Murphy: Village People and Yothu Yindi drummer

Dear Dad

Are you dead yet?

My sister and I have waited over 30 years to be free from you, and I heard you've been unwell. I had a brief moment of elation when your lawyer called last year, but it was only you wanting something back that you'd put in our names. I'm not sure why you thought we'd want to help. You never even paid child support.

You don't know this: when I was younger, I wanted to be a gymnast. The classes cost five dollars a week, but Mum couldn't afford it. If you had chosen to assist, this is what the money would have been spent on. That and a new school uniform, then I wouldn't have had to scrounge jumpers and sports uniforms from the lost property bin so we didn't get detention.

I want you to know that I was sitting behind the front door the day you came to the house and punched Mum in the face. I was only three but I can still see the cut above her left eyebrow. I thought you'd cut her with a knife. I remember the day you took a sledgehammer to our front door and the car window, leaving glass shattered over my baby brother's car seat.

During the same-sex marriage debate, some people justified their view by saying a child deserves a mother and a father. I was born with one of each, but I did nothing to deserve you. The anxiety of being stalked and harassed my entire life doesn't go away. I want to be free.

So I ask again, are you dead yet?

Nikki

Nikki Moyes: young-adult fiction author

Dear Dads

It's complicated, as I had two fathers.

To my natural one. You did what you could with an eighteen-year-old girlfriend you knocked up in the 1950s, living in a strict Catholic atmosphere in a NSW country town. I was adopted out, but you went on to marry her anyway. You had five more kids with her, so thanks for loving my mother so well and for so long.

I only met you twice in the year before you died, but I sensed you loved a chat, a drink, a smoke. And women. You had many careers in your life: prospector, sparky, childcare centre manager, and more. We are similar because you were a gypsy, and the life of a musician would have suited you well. I got that wanderlust from you. You were a rock'n'roller without the rock'n'roll.

I have no animosity about being given up because I see it all through the prism of love, and history can't be changed. It's all sliding doors in the end. It was the times. Thanks for giving me my life.

To my adoptive father. You were a suburban businessman, Dad, and a man of few words. You would stare silently into the fire that you had set in the backyard incinerator on a Sunday and I would secretly watch from behind the hedge. You would pour petrol onto grass clippings and the explosion would shake the windows of the house. Then you would stare some more, lost in unreadable thoughts.

Thanks for doing such a good job in bringing me up. I'm happy I told you as much, weeks before you died, as kids can be ungrateful, and it was because I had children then that I knew a little bit of what it must have been like for you.

Thanks for your attendances: for the knee scrapes, for the school awards nights, for the sausages you would cremate on the barbecue, and for being the breadwinner.

In the end, the one who was there the most is the real dad, and that's what you were.

Jim

Jim Moginie: founding member of Midnight Oil, Grammy nominee and ARIA Hall of Fame inductee

Dear Dad

A salesman came to our house. Tough decisions were made. Today, you can buy a set of 1989 World Books on Gumtree for $100. Or you can get them for free, pick-up only, in the Adelaide Hills. In today's money, you and Mum spent about five thousand dollars on a set of encyclopaedias, produced in Merchandise Mart Plaza in Chicago, for my older sister and me. My daughter is about the age I would have been when those boxes were delivered to our house in Toowoomba. The paper was semi-gloss and edged in gold. All those pictures inside. All that knowledge.

You finished Year Twelve at Southport State High and got a job, and then another. I remember watching you at the pine desk beside our bookshelf, finishing TAFE assignments after your day at work. We had Paterson, Lawson, Park. We had Reader's Digests, *The Richest Man in Babylon*, Tom Clancy. And taking up two shelves – all those dark-green and cream volumes – were the World Books. That's how kids did assignments, as you know. I did a project on the Triceratops.

I did one on the blue whale. I did one on Greece. Population: 10 million. Currency: the drachma.

Once, after dinner, I announced that I would read from an encyclopaedia every night. I'd start at A and soon enough I'd be at Z, and then I would know everything there was to know. I asked if anyone wanted to join little old insufferable me in this lively activity. I opened up the first volume (Alvar Aalto, aardvark, Abaco Islands). Then you came and sat on the other couch, reading silently from B.

Love,

Laura

Laura Elvery: academic and writer

Dear Dad

Update from the Gabagaba ... sitting here in the house it's about 1 am. Can't sleep coz there's a puppy next door that sounds like a dying cat. Probably hungry or got a fishbone stuck in its throat.

Not much changes in the village ... except family keeps growing ... kids getting taller and there's always more of them every time I look.

I'm heading to Port Moresby tomorrow morning to meet with the TV network about a music series we're producing. I'll probably catch a ride into town with Uncle Bondi.

I saw Aunty Jenny today and dropped off the materials Mum gave me to give to her, so she can make more *bilums* for Lele to sell in Brisbane. She's also making a new *puriki* basket. It's a good initiative to raise money for her medical expenses, but she is going to need a truckload more to raise enough, because the hospital here is so expensive.

Uncle Kule and Aunty Margi came over tonite for some *bakibaki* which Bubu Vasira and Nelly (Moki's daughter) cooked.

Bakibaki's never been my favourite ... but it's what you eat when the only thing in the cupboard is flour and tinned fish.

Caught up with Debs, too, about family reunion plans for Christmas here. Hopefully we can save up enough money to bring everyone. It's about time our generation is more proactive about keeping the unity in our family. They've just returned from Gaire village tonight. One of Uncle Basil's *bubus* passed away from leukaemia. He was only six. So sad to hear about it, coz he was so young, and the father was working away from home as a school teacher in Sepik. Doctors advised the parents to not bother with their fundraising efforts as it was too late ... I can't imagine hearing that.

It seems every day is so jam-packed here in PNG. The movie we're working on is off to a good start. I met the fellas in Moresby after their recce trip down the Sepik River, Morobe coastline and around the streets of Lae. Funny how one thing leads to another here in PNG ... it all started with a song, which led to a canoe voyage, which led to the creation of Mo-Arts, which is a new arts-based NGO in Lae, which created the Dua Dua Festival, which led to the revival of *Kasali*, the ancient trade canoe from Buingim, and now the movie. That song definitely has a life force of its own.

Anyways, this dog next door still going ... I might go see what's up with it ... before a non-dog person does.

Love to you and Mum.

See you soon,

Airi

Airi Ingram: percussionist, composer and producer

Dear Dad

Let's get this straight, you loved me. I was your 'little fella' and in fourteen short years we had some life-changing times. You stood by as I caught my first fish, a little carp, on a sandy bank of the river. The night before we had slumbered in our sleeping bags, laid out on dry clay near tall gum trees. We had a blanket of stars above that went on forever, and I knew that I was loved.

You were my hockey coach, and in our premiership year you showed me how to play a few positions. Centre, wing, inner, full-back and goalie; you gave me a go. To this day, defence is my natural strength.

When I was nine years old you diligently taught me how to drive a tractor, and I recall your 'emergency stop!' Immediately I'd hit the brakes, shove the gearstick into neutral and turn the engine off. Despite that huge red machine being too big for me, I felt safe.

I loved the blue go-cart that never did have the Victa mower engine fitted; instead, you tied a rope to our farm truck and towed me down a dirt road. Full of joy, my spirit soared as I slid and bumped, coming to a rolling stop under the shade of a willow tree near the shed.

Life, though, isn't perfect. And yes, some scars remain raw. When I dwell for too long on those traumas, I breathe, see through the dark and find the light so as not to cloud everything and suck the beauty from our good times together.

But letting a twelve-year-old drive you home after a party when you were pissed, or sitting me at the bar with lemonade as you drank beer, well, that now feels weird. Nights on my knees praying that you'd make it home safely when I knew that you were out after work, drinking. And you'd drive home.

One time it didn't work out, and that was a morning in July when big brother Chris woke me, saying: 'There's been an accident and Dad is dead.' I'll never know what drove your recklessness. One too many times speeding in the car in a mood that descended like a dark cloud, and your number was up. Something else had a hold of you then.

In my moments of despair, I've played copy-cat and driven like the devil with one eye on a dire outcome, too. Thankfully, through the grace of God, those thoughts don't plague me anymore. I've got too much to live for. I don't view you through rose-coloured glasses and pretend that everything was okay; you did the best with what you were given.

But know that my love runs deep and so much of what we did was built on love.

Love,

Nick

Nick Bennett: journalist, broadcaster and voice-over guy

Dear Dad

Once upon a time a young Dutchman was tired of being cold, so he sailed across the world, met a lovely young woman, and two days later proposed to her. Before long, they had a tribe of children and built themselves a house at the edge of a forest.

At night he would tell stories to his kids about a cold northern land full of trolls and magic and giants and clever children. When it stormed, he'd gather them behind the curtains to gasp at lightning and laugh at thunder. On clear moonless nights, they'd lie on the roof and he'd tell stories about the stars. He'd take them into the forest, the smallest on his shoulders, the rest scrambling behind as he strode long-legged through the bush, singing and telling them about the trees, the birds and the animals.

He'd take them driving, and the children would beg him to get lost again. He'd laugh and turn up random lanes and tracks, pointing out kangaroos and cows and clouds that looked like dragons, or like tanks because he remembered the war, and they'd drink it all in, wondering with delicious dread, like Hansel and Gretel, if they'd find their way home.

Nowadays, Dad, as you sit in your armchair in the house you built with your own hands, chatting to the people on the TV screen, you're not always sure who we are, these kids who followed you like the Pied Piper and absorbed your love of the natural world.

But we know who you are, and we always will.

We'll love you forever, Dad.

Joanne

Joanne van Os: radio operator, bull catcher, buffalo station owner, home schooling teacher, electorate officer, boat hire owner/operator, cartoonist, writer

Dear Dad

I'm still not sure how this cosmos/eternal-life/heaven/God business works, but if it does turn out the way most of us are hoping then you have a fairly good idea that I think about you pretty much every day – often many times a day. And of course on Father's Day you get Maximum Thoughts (MT).

Usually my thoughts are triggered by little things: old books of yours that I see daily on my shelves; the way the wind's blowing; something Mum says. Or maybe something she doesn't say. But her thoughts, and mine, linger in the air.

You know I've checked in on her every day since you passed away. It used to be 3 pm but she gets a bit tired by then and is much better in the mornings, so I call at 11 am. But I'm guessing you know that. I'm sorta relaxed to imagine you might be listening in on our calls. We never say anything bad.

It's footy season again as I write this, and I often think of you taking me week in and week out to watch East Launceston play when I was around ten. Me and my mass of red, white and blue streamers on that big stick I used to wave whenever we kicked a goal. That was when I was outside with you. Often we'd sit in the car together – especially after a drive to Scottsdale or another country game – and keep warm watching from the front seat. How cool was it being able to drive the car right up to the fence at these games? Very cool is how cool! And remember the year East Launceston won the premiership? And you took me into the rooms after the game and I managed to get the whole team to sign my footy record? So many memories, Dad.

But you know what I think about most? I wish I'd been as good at this Dad business as you were. I'm still working on that.

Miss you and love you, Dad.

Stuart

Stuart Coupe: rock group manager, music journalist and promoter

Dear Dad

Well it's nineteen years from there to here, since flesh and blood became whatever to this quiet remembering. Mind you, the remembering thing happens more often than you'd think, especially each time our youngest son knocks at the door … 'Shave and a haircut – two bits!' Your signature is safe in his hands. Funny the things that last.

And how, at every family get-together, when your famous cue comes down from the rack, the stories roll off each boy's tongue of one grand time they beat you to the eight ball. How sweet it was, knowing, until some controversial call, you were definitely going to win. It's a beautiful thing, laughter, even if it's at your expense.

On a sadder note, vintage 2000 reds are getting scarce. A bottle for each anniversary eventually takes its toll on the cellar, and the angel's share has certainly decreased with all these grandkids raising a glass in your direction now. I've actually taken to savouring your portion myself after everyone goes home. Sorry about that, but you were never one to waste a drop.

Also, while I'm 'fessing up, I've made mileage out of you on several occasions when after-dinner conversation turned to politics. I break out that story about the first time I got to cast my vote. It was post Whitlam's sacking and I brazenly threatened to vote Liberal! You were apoplectic; what was it you said? 'Traitor To Your People!' Of course it always gets a laugh, but looking back it was a cruel joke to play on a man who believed so passionately in social justice.

Now before I go, I've been wrestling with a song for you for a while, but can't seem to get around to finishing it. Maybe subconsciously I'm afraid it will bring about some kind of closure, and we don't need or want that, do we? Let me know what you think. It opens …

My dad was a railway man
the railway was his life
My mum a railway widow
like every railway wife
and all his friends were railway men
and all were proud to be
life-time ticket holders
of the A.F.U.L.E.

'Til next time,

G

Graeme Connors: vocalist for Kris Kristofferson and Sherbet, songwriter for Slim Dusty, John Denver and Jon English

Dear Dad

I got to Melbourne safely, and my trip couldn't have gone better. All those epic road trips you took us on as kids have instilled in me an unshakeable love of the road. Not to mention the adventures in the truck, when we would grab our sleeping bags at three in the morning and clamber up into the cab with you for the eight-hour haul to Adelaide, sitting so high up, the diesel engine rumbling and warm underneath us, headlights slicing through the cold night ahead.

I am so grateful for this legacy, Dad, that I love the road as much as I do. Because as a singer/songwriter, travelling is a big part of the job.

On my dashboard I have kept the note you left on my driver's seat before I headed off. It brought a tear to my eye when I read it. Written in your instantly recognisable capital letters. Always saying just enough, not one syllable too many. A man of few words, you've never been one to mince them:

HEADLIGHT GLOBE

FITTED TEST OK

BRAKE FLUID ADDED

TYRE PRESSURES

CHECKED AND ADJUSTED

SAFE TRAVEL

LOVE YOU,

DAD

That little note says so much; it speaks of your belief in me, your complete confidence that I will successfully execute this latest adventure. As much as you want me to be safe, it illustrates how you've always made me feel free, and encouraged me to follow my dreams. This humble little note is symbolic of your steadfast support, symbolic of your love.

I can't thank you enough, Dad – and this is only scratching the surface.

I love you. I hope you know how much.

Love,

Jodi

Jodi Martin: songwriter

Dear Dad

Thank you, for everything! For your love, for the security, comfort and advice (not always taken) you provided. Thank you for having the vision to encourage me to become a chef. Thank you for your belief in me.

Life was never easy for you, Dad; I can't imagine what you and Mum went through when you lost such a loving daughter (my sister), but still, you always put your family first. I look back at your emotion, tears of sadness, tears of joy … all yours, Dad, true love and emotion. That has made me what I am today, Dad.

You saw things before I saw them; you were a great judge of character. If only I had listened to you … but I knew better. How wrong I was! I am stronger now, thanks to you.

It's been 22 years since we last spoke. To this day, Dad, I love you and miss you; I thank you, for moulding me to be the best I can be for my children. I love you, Dad. Your son,

Athol xxx

Athol Wark: executive chef, wild food expert

Dear Dad

It would be much easier for me to write this letter as a song, but that's already been done. Already I'm talking music ... and I have you to thank for that. Since I can remember, and at no particular time of the day, I could hear the sounds of a foot stomping on a kitchen floor and gentle chords playing from the squeezebox. Then the song, a song that you thought had a great beat and great lyrics.

I remember the silly songs and us kids laughing and joining in. But I guess the biggest lesson I learnt from you was the ability to hear music. It's only now that I understand it's a really cool way to play. When I hear the song I can direct its journey because I already hear it in front of me. '*Prop it up, twitch of wire, teach me how a motor fires ... and teach me how to cry when a useless dog dies.*'

Dad, you taught us so much, but most importantly you taught us to look out for each other. We are all still so close today, and I rely on family so much.

I sincerely hope that your philosophy has rubbed off on me and Dave and that I can teach our four boys to shake hands and bear hug 'til the end. Our Bill is just like you. So when your time in this shell is up and I'm missing you, I'll just give him a hug and hear the music.

Love you Dad,

Sara x

PS Thank you for not stopping at three kids, because I'm having the best bloody life.
PPS This sounds really morbid, I know, but can you visit me after you're gone? It has to be a bird ... you choose! A Mallee galah might suit?

Sara Storer: country muso, 21 Golden Guitars

Dear Dad

It's late Thursday night and I'm sitting in my lounge room. I've decided to write to you, inspired by the cover of a book on my coffee table. I didn't notice it before, but it has thin lines drawn around the edges of the cover. It reminded me of the thin lines around the go-cart you built for David and me.

Do you remember? My little brother and I tried to build one, but it was impossible. It must have been a Saturday afternoon, or maybe it was a Sunday. I remember you painted blue lines around the edges of the cart and around the seat with a piece of dowelling under your arm to keep that small paintbrush steady. I didn't know that painting blue lines around the edges of the go-cart could have such a beautiful effect.

I have always remembered your attention to detail. This go-cart was not just slapped together. It was designed, measured and built using tools we'd never seen before. Every piece of wood was shaped, planed and sanded down. We were too young to be of any real help, but you still made us feel that we were helping.

We both watched as the cart became a living reality, right before our eyes. You had materialised a magnificent vehicle out of junk found under the house: planks of timber, old silver-spoked pram wheels, and some rope. I remember you made two steel axles, and found a bolt for the steering mechanism. You turned an old cupboard drawer into a seat for us to sit in. When you first fixed it to the cart I remember you asked us to test the seat. David and I sat in it like we were travelling at the speed of sound, pretending we were roaring down the hill in the nearby park. We suddenly realised we were going to need a helmet for speeds as great as this machine could produce – at least 40 kilometres per hour on a steep hill.

Today was a long day for me, and I'm a bit tired. Perhaps that's why I noticed the thin lines on the book. To me they represent the love and effort you built into that go-cart. I wanted to say thanks for the go-cart, and thanks for the blue lines.

Charlie

Charlie Rooke: composer, session guitarist, instrumental teacher and founder of '90s rock act The Sharp

Dear sillybilly,[#]

I hated your letter (that's only a gok). Today I went to a speshel place with dinasors. I cut and pasted this picture for you. I am doing well in scool. I play with my frens after scool some times. It has been very hot here. The class room gets very hot too.

Love me.

***

Dear Daddy,

Tomorrow is a holiday because it is the queen's birthday. I just thot I would right you a letter sins I wasn't doing anything.

Love Clare

PS I got my hair cut.

***

Saterday 30.7.77

Dear Dad

I got the stuffed animals (I adore them). The wether here is teroble. I have some new textas whitch I am writing with. I have a lose tooth now.

Love you know who

P.S I have a riddle (what did the pink-panther say when he steped on the ant? dead-ant dead-ant dead-ant dead-ant dead-ant dead-ant)

***

16 Feb 1979

Dear Dad

I don't want to worry you, but I'm sick. I may have my tonsils out. On the May holidays we are proply going to Hawaii. We already have tickets. I love you.

Clare

***

12 May 1982 (only two days until I'm a teenager!!!)

Dear Dad

Well, it's now school holidays so I finally have a bit of time to write a nice long letter. I really love school but it's so GREAT to be able to not worry about homework and getting to bed early (11pm). I know this sounds late but I've found that if I go to bed any earlier I only lie awake for hours which drives me cookoo. Tomorrow Bill and I and Mandy and Richard are going to the movies as sort of a pre-birthday party. From Mum and John I'm getting tennis lessons, a tracksuit and a big raise in my allowance (from $2 to $5). Lately I've been spending a lot of money, mainly on clothes but also going out, buying records etc ...

All my love, Clare

25.9.85

Dearest, darling Dad,

It's going to be great when I live in Canada for my gap year. For some reason I think we'll fight a lot. The reason I think we'll fight a lot is because we're both quite emotional people. I also think we'll fight because we're going to be in the position of having to face real life together (not holiday fun times) and not having lived together and worked each other out over a long period of time. Problem areas (probably): drinking, sex, grass. We'll test each other for a while, but she'll be right mate.

Clare xoxoxoxo

***

19.5.93

Dearest Dad,

Lunchtime, and I'm indulging in a small pizza on Lygon St. This opportunity to escape the claustrophobia (geographical and social) of my new office job and to sit at a window table in the early winter sun is truly worthy of indulgence. As you might have gathered, my new job is not crash hot ...

Love, Clare

***

27 November 1996

Dad:

It's Thursday, and the first time I have been at uni (and thus on an email-friendly computer) for two weeks. Once we both get on the Net at our respective homes (one of these days), the real advantages of this form of communication can be realised.

The baby in my tum is very active these days – kicking, somersaulting, doing whatever a babe in utero does to keep busy. It is a weird and wonderful feeling. Have you thought any more about coming out next year, oh-soon-to-be-grandfatherly one?

Love,

C. Alice Wright (joke)

My dad and I were separated by the Pacific Ocean in 1974, when I was five years old. He lived in Canada; I lived in Australia, with my mother and new stepfather, John. Dad and I bridged the gulf through copious, endless letter-writing. A platform for love across the seas. My letters almost always started 'Dear Dad'.

Associate Professor Clare Wright: author, broadcaster, academic

Dear Dad

It's been almost three years since I last saw your face, and all the photographs in the world don't seem to make the grief any easier to bear. There are so many things to tell you, and I spend too much time writing you emails in my head which end up just floating away into nothing.

I wanted to thank you for being such a wonderful father. Yes, you had your flaws, as we all do, but for a man who had only ever grown up with a brother and whose relationship with your own father ended at eighteen when he died, you did such a great job of raising me and my three sisters.

Your presence was hard to describe to anyone who didn't know you. When you entered a room, people stopped talking to hear what you had to say. You rarely raised your voice. You didn't need to – people flowed towards you to listen. With a simple clearing of your throat, conversations stilled and heads turned expectantly. You spoke volumes without saying a word.

Your blue eyes, when angry, could freeze over. Somehow you managed to convey your displeasure with just that look – steely enough to make an obnoxious teenager rethink.

Your laugh was full-throated and from the belly. You had a dark and twisty sense of humour and it was hard to make you laugh, but when you did laugh it felt like the whole world tilted on its axis, laughing with you. Even when the jokes were terrible, and they often were.

You taught me about honour. An old-fashioned word for these modern times, but you had it in bucketfuls. You were the man in his eighties who took the long flight (that likely killed you) in order that your eldest daughter and your granddaughters could navigate an ugly divorce with love standing behind them

You adored my daughters. Where others saw cheekiness, you saw spirit. You always spoke to them as if they were mini adults and, as children often do, they saw that you were being a real person – no pretence. You were never afraid to be silly or affectionate with them. You were their one true positive male role model, and I know that without you in their lives their views regarding men might have become seriously twisted.

You taught me about love. You loved my mother so much, and despite having waited and worked and waited and worked until your retirement so that you and she could travel, her Parkinson's meant that you only ever managed a couple of visits with her to see my family. You took good care of her all your married life, and when the dementia worsened, you managed and coped as best you could for as long as you could, alone.

You gave me courage. You were the first person I ever told that I had Stage IV breast cancer and that the prognosis wasn't good. I remember the long pause at your end of the phone line and then you cleared your throat and simply said, 'I'm so sorry, Louise. But we will get through this together, you are not alone.'

There's so much I want to thank you for, Dad, on this Father's Day, but the sad reality is that you are gone and all those missed chances to tell you that I loved you and that I admired you have vanished along with you. So this Father's Day, I will write another imaginary email and send it to you *wherever* you are; as if you still *are*; and hope that, by some quirk of fate, you realise what a huge gaping hole you've left in my life.

I loved you, Dad. I love you Dad.

Lou

Louise Munnoch: patient advocate at Love Your Sister

Dear Dad

It's been a long time since I've written you a letter or sent you a card. I miss being able to do that, especially on Father's Day.

Fourteen years have flown by, and every day without you has stacked up like a pile of unread books ... stories you should have been a part of but weren't here to share. I'm sure you're busy on the other side. I'm assuming you're the official pastry cook upstairs, baking heavenly pies and the best bread that side of the pearly gates.

You were a beautiful soul in this world, mostly. Sometimes you were a stubborn old bastard, but I'm sure you're still touching hearts in the next. If you can find the time to drop by, between baking and travelling the universe, that would be great. I'll be having a scotch on Father's Day, thinking of you. If you feel like a chat, I'll be the slightly inebriated one talking to thin air. Love always,

Lynette

Lyn Bowtell: seven times Golden Guitar winner

Dear Dad

Here are some things I haven't told you before, because I think the longest we've ever spoken on the phone is about fifteen minutes. It's nothing serious; I haven't done drugs (actually, I did once) or gotten a tattoo (although I've been thinking about it and hoping your attitude towards ink has changed), and I'm not pregnant (not a priority for me at this stage, but I think one day you'd make a fun Gong Gong). I just want to thank you for some things that you might not think I remember, or maybe at the time you thought were insignificant, but were significant to me.

Thanks for the bizarre assortment of food you'd bring me when you picked me up from school – the Filet-o-Fish meals, apple Danishes and curry pies from the bakery, the bottles of Bundaberg ginger beer and the takeaway containers full of roasted cashews. (Thanks also for always picking me up early.)

Thanks for staying up and drawing with me after your late-night shifts at work when I stayed over at your house (when you lived at the Asian markets).

Thanks for letting me crash at your place when I was broken-hearted for the first time, and for offering advice and insisting on giving up your bed and sleeping on the couch, even though you had a bad leg.

Thanks for passing on your ambitiousness and tendency to daydream to me, and for always supporting whatever I've wanted to do. You've given me the space to carve my own path and you've trusted that I'll always be okay.

These are some, but not all, of my thankyous. (The next ones will go in a card!) But they're worth noting, because I think a lot of the time you felt like you could have been better, and that you didn't know what you were doing, which is something I'm understanding more as I get older. I get it. I'm thankful for you and I love you, Dad.

Love,

Mum

敏儀

Michelle Law: writer (Sh*t Asian Mothers Say*), *AWGIE award winner*

Dear Dad

What can I say? Only that you're the most amazing man ever. You've been the epitome of what a dad is. I couldn't have been more blessed than the blessing of you in our lives.

I often hear the question, What does a dad mean to you? Especially around Father's Day. I'm lucky to say that every day is Father's Day because of you.

Though you are not my biological father, your blood still covers me as if you were. You never made me feel anything but love, and your wisdom resonates within me every day. You unselfishly have poured into my sister and me an abundance of love, and you show that love to our mother over and over again.

Never have I experienced one like you, and to experience you in my life can only be what God intended. Thank you for loving me and, most of all, THANK YOU for showing me that men like you exist. I love you Dad!

MsMo

Ms Monét: singer

Dear Dad

Thanks for failing to pass down any of your painting or drawing talents to me. The first time I became aware of this was when I drew a pathetic-looking horse and became the laughing stock of my primary school art class. Even the teacher couldn't quite make out what type of animal it was. Somehow I then realised there was a weight of expectation upon me to be good, which made the whole thing terribly humiliating. I was only seven, for God's sake. I remember thinking that day what an absolute prick you were.

All I've ever wanted to do is to be able to express myself eloquently on canvas. You knew this was my dream, probably even back when I was a tiny foetus kicking around in Mum's belly. So, what is your problem? It appears you have blessed my three other siblings with the ability to express themselves remarkably as painters, yet somehow you decided to skip me. How can you live with yourself?

Look, I know it's not really *all* your fault, and I do have to give you some credit for keeping a dignified silence regarding my overall lack of artistic talent. However, as your son I feel it is my duty to blame you. You simply could have done better.

So I guess I need to use this opportunity to say thanks publicly. Thanks for making me the official dud of the family. Arsehole.

You did this deliberately.

Love from your frustrated artist son,

Sunny

PS My therapist tells me that excluding me from any family drawing skills has done irreparable damage to my psyche. Please don't feel bad about this in any way.

Sunny Leunig: magosopher (a rare crossbreed of magician and philosopher)

Dear Dad

I know you don't like it here. This place, with its 'carers' and 'clients', bland meals and euphemisms. It's tough being away from your family – away from Mum, especially, after almost 60 years. Your world has shrunk to fit a disease, not the life you've led.

Some time ago your precious, difficult mind turned enemy, the worst betrayal. It's left you with loneliness and fear, as you drift away from yourself, from us.

Words have now failed you, but there's still a spark in your eyes, a connection to us, our past. Let's visit some forgotten places. Squeeze my hand, close your eyes – we'll go together.

We'll go yabbying on the farm all those years ago, with the dogs running loose on a hot summer's day. We'll stay in the house you built for us, brick by brick, with its Italian arches and cool, tiled floors. We'll have dinner together, Mum and the four boys, our whole family.

In your entire life you've never been frightened of anything or anyone, and you've never, ever backed down. It's driven us crazy sometimes. But, like all of us, you'll have to back down, eventually. And I hope I'll be there. I'll hold your hand, just like this, and we'll remember better days. Because touch is our mother tongue, the first language we learn, the last we rely on.

Because in the end, words aren't so important. Because sometimes, Dad, words fail me too.

Mark

Mark Brandi: award-winning crime writer

Dear Dad

I appreciate you not killing me as a child. I don't know how you didn't!

I did think that by now I would have heard at least one song from your band, Max the Rockers, that you told us kids about. I'm still waiting. I'm starting to think you might have made it all up.

But seriously, thanks for being my best mate, my idol, my biggest supporter, my ear for advice, my life mentor and, most of all, thanks for always having my back. I can always count on you when I need a hand with anything.

We have shared some of the best memories together, which I will never forget for as long as I live. I wouldn't be the man or fighter I am today without the support and guidance you gave me. I have learned some great life lessons from you and tried to mould myself based upon them.

I do hope one day you can have a win with one of your fights, so when someone asks where I got my fighting ability from, you can say your normal, 'Yeah, I was pretty good,

I had thirty-six fights, forty losses.' Then you can add a win in there, too, lol.

You're a legend, mate. Thanks for everything. Thanks for being my dad. Catch you for a few froffies soon, Chief!

From your son and best mate,

Jason

Jason Whateley: four times Australian Boxing Heavyweight Champion and qualified butcher

Dear Dad

Happy what-would-have-been-your-70th birthday. I went to Midland Cemetery on the weekend. Each time I visit, new headstones have appeared all around yours. This year, one of the new headstones bears the inscription, *If love could have saved you, you would have lived forever.*

We had a murky meeting in a dream shortly after you died. I think I asked you why you had to leave. You said, *I was tired.*

I don't know what it was like to have lived like you did, that final year. Having liquid dinner poured down a tube into your stomach, spitting into tissues. The sleepless chokehold of coughing fits. The boredom of it all.

I used to be sick in a different way. You tried to ask me about it once. How could I tell you about lying awake at night, wondering how quickly I might die if I drove into a lake, or about the time I sat in my car at uni and hit myself with my phone, over and over, in the skin above my heart. I was tired.

I know that pain can get so bad that it doesn't matter who loves you, or who you'd leave behind. I'm not saying that our pain was identical or comparable. Just that I understand that pain can exceed all the love in the world. You didn't die from not loving or being loved hard enough.

Surely your goodness and love will follow me all the days of my life, says one of your epitaph's inscriptions. I hope goodness and love have followed you to where you are now, a place where life cannot hurt you any more.

Elizabeth

Elizabeth Tan: webcomic, writer

Dear Dad

Sometimes I wonder what I'd say if I was lucky enough to see you again. Realistically, it'd probably be something along the lines of, 'Holy shit, ghosts are *real*?' or, 'Dammit, does this mean I'm dead now?' Maybe I wouldn't say anything at all. Yeah. I'd just hug you.

Sometimes I wish you'd been able to die a year earlier than you did, just like you wanted. It's been eleven years now, and I still think about you every day. I miss your voice – your real voice – the voice you had before the cancer took it away. I miss standing in front of you while you fixed my tie (because I never got it right). I miss seeing you meticulously butter every square centimetre of your toast. I miss your obsession with the weather. I miss being out on the farm with you, and seeing you with Mum. Hell, sometimes I even miss feeding you, shaving you, putting you to bed and helping you dress, because as horrible as that time was, at least we were all together. Nobody should have to go through what you did. I'm sorry we couldn't save you.

You always told me, 'Be good, be wise,' and I'm trying. That first chapter I made you read before you died? It's an actual book now.

I've travelled. I've loved and been loved. Oh, and I'm gay, by the way. Surprise! There's so much we never got to talk about, never got to say, even though we knew what was coming.

I'll write you another letter soon. For now, it's back to work, which I know is what you really want to hear.

Much love,

Jem

Jeremy Lachlan: author, karaoke wannabe

Dear Dad

Thanks for falling in love with me when I was a useless shitting baby lump, and not reneging as I grew into a more complicated human being. It's really helped me out.

Thanks, also, for never letting me win at anything, for playing 'boy' sports with me, for teaching me the word 'fartlek' when I was only eleven (I found it funny then and I find it funny now). Thanks for saving me from drowning, twice, and for letting me climb really high trees, even after I fell out of them. Thanks for reading to me, for reading everything I've ever written, for giving me the capability and strength to argue with you. Whenever we asked you the meaning of a word, you'd say, 'It's good to ask questions.' Thanks for driving us and picking us up; for pushing us, accepting us, delighting in us; for giving father-ness to friends and family who needed it. Thanks for trying desperately to teach me not to swear. (Maybe that taught *you* a lesson: you sure can't win at everything, bucko.) Thanks for teaching us to be seekers, to be playful, to be curious. Thanks for showing us how good it is to move your body. Thanks for always being in the crowd.

Thanks for finding our mum, for loving her for a while. And thanks for finding the guts to tell me she had died.

You once showed me an old Super 8 home movie where I'm playing 'What's the Time Mr Wolf?' with you and Mum. We're in an idyllic North American forested campsite wearing matching Bellbrae Primary School jumpers. I'm Mr Wolf, obvs, because I'm three and require attention at all times.

I watched it over and over. I couldn't stop looking at your face. It was so full of – and there's no other word for it, nothing less corny than this – *love* for me.

It seems unfair that you don't get to remember the moment your dad falls in love with you, that you don't get to see the moment your parents fall in love with each other, that you don't get to see the reason for your own aliveness.

But it's just the way it works.

Thanks for it all, Dad. I love being your daughter.

Love,

Brooke

Brooke Davis: author (translated into 20 languages)

Dear Dad

My connection to you and to fatherhood has not been smooth. But, rocky as it has been, three men in my childhood have been towering role models for me. I want to tell you about them.

You left Mum after eight years of marriage, leaving her to raise sons aged seven, five and four. In a housing trust home in Hectorville. She was the dad, the mum, and all the other roles.

You were a 'career' alcoholic by the age of 50. Yes, there were many understandable reasons for that. You did not receive enough love in your own childhood. You had two or three stepfathers and one was unspeakably cruel. You were shuffled between divorced parents.

Enter, Uncle Neville. Mum's only sister married Nev, the eldest of thirteen, from a Mallee farm near Karoonda, South Australia. He served in Darwin as a nineteen-year-old during the war. He later ran his own building business, employing up to 70 people, and became a mayor. He was captain–coach of the church footy team at the age of 42. Talk about a solid

Australian. He's been Lions president and captain of the bowls team – it's like he's captained everything. He's currently 96, and to quote one of your best expressions: 'You can't shoot him.' The story goes he would ride a bike about ten kilometres across the suburbs with lengths of timber held on his shoulder – to get the work done.

Uncle Neville stepped in where we three brothers lacked a dad. When I was thirteen he very graciously offered to take me to a sex education evening. We went to a hall with a screen and projector, and it showed an illustration of the male part inside the female part. I recall thinking, *Crikey! Is THAT how it's done!*

As we three boys traversed our teens, Uncle Nev was the father figure we so needed. And he did it entirely selflessly and humbly. He never imposed, intruded, overstepped. He only quietly did the right thing at the right time, always.

Two other men stepped up: two dads from two neighbouring families. Max, across the road, was a motorbike policeman. As upright as they come! Max helped guide us three urchins when we needed it – and we did. He taught each of us to drive, and gave up so much time for us.

Mark, also across the road, was another role model. Both Max and Mark were raising families; Mark had four kids, Max two. Mark worked at the GMH car plant. When I was trying to keep my battling 1952 Morris Minor going – which Mum had heroically bought me when I was still sixteen – Mark stepped up. To keep the Morrie Minor on the road I replaced the diff, a head gasket, the piston rings, did a valve re-grind – everything. But who guided me on how to do it? Mark. The tiny valve guides and cotter pins were too hard for me. So I would wait for Mark to get home from work, and he would be sitting at his kitchen table having a longneck, talking to his wife Joan, in his own housing trust home. I would sheepishly ask if he would come over and help me work out how to put the valves back in. He would pause – the LAST thing he needed after a hot day and a trip to the Woodville factory was bending over a greasy motor ... and he would say he'd be over directly.

He would finish the longneck, stroll over and stick his head under the bonnet with a torch to find the tiny valve guides. What a hero. I haven't forgotten you, Mark.

There are some fond memories I have of you, Dad. You loved music, kept a drum kit in the corner, and you dug your Gene Krupa – you were a hi-fi buff – like your own dad. The one record of yours I adored most, and which I was kindly given after you died, was Frank Sinatra and Antônio Carlos Jobim's Latin collaboration album. You and I shared a deep love for that record.

You had another expression that I will hang on to until my grave. When we spoke by phone of our joy at the turning of winter to spring, you said, 'You can feel the sap rising in your bones.' Never a truer word was spoken.

Greg

Greg Champion: Coodabeen Champion for 36 years, Greg Champion has released over 30 CDs, and by his own admission has a few gongs in the VMI category: 'Vaguely Minor Identity'. Greg grew up in the Hectorville Home For The Visually Unpleasant, and nowadays does guest speaking, where he's classified as a De-Motivational Speaker. A four-time runner-up in the Australian Underachiever Awards, Champs has no criminal record.

Dear Dad

Remember those sepia-stained summers when I was a kid? They were kinda carefree. The only potential risk I faced was being invisible – being the only girl, unremarkable, small, and the middle child and all.

But Dad, you gave me a ripper gift that changed all that. It was '77. Elvis had just carked it and his records were on high rotation. Back then our only entertainment was leaping through the oscillating sprinkler, or playing out on the street until tea time.

My big brother had ditched his crusty blue and yellow scooter. He left it like a fallen soldier on the hot concrete. Like most eleven-year-olds he'd upgraded to a Dragster and I felt left out as he sped off with his mates.

Well, Dad, you scooped up that dejected old scooter, carried it into the garage and spray-painted it glossy purple, just for me. I can still hear the hiss of the can and the acrid smell of paint as you bent over the metal frame. Once the paint had dried, I rolled my new wheels out into the 'hood with all the valour of a Valkyrie. Oh, the joy of hooning down the hill, the northerly whipping through my bowl-cut; the pleasure of beating those pimply boys on their bikes!

You see, Dad, that summer you didn't just give me a scooter before upcycling was a thing. You made me feel important ... and just a little bit cool. That gift has hung around. Just like the faded purple silhouette of a scooter on the garage floor.

Love,

Elise

X

Elise Elliott: TV journalist, news host and political correspondent

Dear Dad

It's been a while since I wrote, so I thought I'd bring you up to speed with what I'm up to. Ben and I started on the new deck yesterday. Ripping up the old, laying out string lines and starting to reuse the merbau. Made me think of you. In fact, every time I do a 'handyman' job, I think of you. Thanks for that. Last week, in just two days I patched some plaster in the spare room, fixed a bathroom cupboard that was off its hinges, and reconnected the grey water pump. There seems to be nothing I won't 'give a go'. Thanks for that.

Do you remember that time, years ago, when I came over and we had a coffee at the Festival Theatre? I got all emotional and said, 'At this rate of visits, I'll only see you ten more times!' And then do you remember what happened? Nothing. Nothing changed. Thanks for that.

That's why I'm doing the backyard makeover with my son. To teach him the skills you taught me, but also to make a space where we can sit down at the end of it and smell the flowers we planted. Mainly thanks to his mum, Ben can talk to anyone, about anything – and he wants to. I can teach him things, but he can teach me more. We are who we are because of the people in our lives. I'm proud I'm your son, and I love you, but I wish we'd stopped and sat more.

I have much to thank you for, Dad, but you didn't give me everything. I don't blame you. I know how hard it is to act against what comes naturally.

Last week was ten years since you died. I don't have any new memories to replace the ones that hurt. So I'll just keep plastering and hammering and be content at that. And sit and chat to Ben. And for all that – I thank you.

Love,

Mike

Michael Pope: voice-over legend, TV all-star

Dear Dad

How I wish you were still here. It is hard to believe you left this earth eighteen years ago. As I write, it is autumn in the beautiful Adelaide hills. The leaves are turning and wood smoke is filling the air as people light their fires for the chilly nights.

This is a special place, a place you introduced us to when we were children, you being an Aldgate Valley boy. It brings a tear to my eye when I pass our dear Heather's home in Stirling; our sister, your daughter, lost too early in life from breast cancer. I hope you, Mum and Heather are together now and that Mum is playing her piano. Your three girls, Marilyn, Heather and I, have always been so grateful to have had such a loving father and mother. Some people aren't so blessed. You encouraged us in all our dreams and wisely taught us many lessons – particularly to be independent, and to buy a property early in our adult lives.

How you would have loved the computer age. It's sad you didn't get to experience it. You were so well-read, learning about the world, people, politics, finance and property. You were forward thinking in telling us everyone could write a book, just as you did; which is held in the National Archives of Australia.

You worked so hard, simultaneously running your own business at night, having a day job, building shops and investing in multiple properties. Your colleagues regarded you as a true gentleman, and they were right.

That's my dad – Sir Reg! You even thanked Mum after every meal she cooked. We used to laugh when you said, what hope did you have with four women in the house? You looked after us all so well. You were very proud of your daughters and each of their achievements. You did everything for your family. We love you Dad.

Beverly

Bev Harrell OAM: pint-sized singer/entertainer with a schooner-sized résumé

Dear Dad

By the time you read this I will be gone ... Not really, I've just always wanted to start a letter with that. Yes, I'm your dickhead son, always have been, always will be, but where do you think I get it from?

I'm trying not to write this letter like it's an obituary, but I'm immediately drawn to talking about all you've taught me and of the happier memories. The truth is, though, my fondest memories aren't of you and me.

They're of you and all the young men you were there for who needed a role model and a friend through their teenage years. You were more than just their football coach, you were Uncle Butch – and still are, well into these young fellas' adult lives.

You've been like a father to many wandering souls, the troubled and lost youth in need of a kindred spirit to keep them on the straight and narrow. To the few who sadly couldn't be saved, to the vast majority who have bloomed and still look up to you as a mentor and friend.

For a lot of years I almost resented the fact that you seemed more concerned with these other kids than your own, at times, but I understand now. My brother and sister and I were the lucky ones, growing up with a mother and father who loved each other and us. We had a roof over our heads, food always on the table and a spoilt upbringing, to say the least.

We weren't abused, we weren't alone, we were just blissfully unaware of how good we had it. I am the luckiest of them all to call you Dad … though I wish I had Mum's hairline :)

With love from your son,

Brad

Brad Butcher: singer/songwriter

Dear Dad

How time flew by! Here I am, not only a father and grandfather myself, but one very near the end of my working life.

My career in the entertainment industry has had highs and lows and much uncertainty, but always a possible future opportunity. It's been more uncertain than I would ever tell you, but it has allowed me to do what I wanted, how I wanted.

This 'how I wanted' has, on reflection, come from accepting and adapting to the lessons in life you gave me. I have no doubt I have hung in in a tough business sector because of the biggest legacy you gave me, the attitude that 'if at first you don't succeed, you try, try again'. As a young one you would often repeat this mantra to me, praise me when I persisted, and let me know very clearly when I gave up too easily.

The other big legacy you left me is the belief that the only way to conduct life is the honest and fair way. This has certainly hindered me at times, when others have outbid me by promising the world and delivering a few grains of sand (I cannot stop thinking about a certain multi-national as I write these words), or not honoured direct commitments made to me (whoops, a couple of names are flooding into my head). The flip side to these behaviours – loyalty, help when needed and the comfort of looking people in the eye – are still the winners. These are lasting assets that will outlive my working career, let me sleep easily at night, and hopefully, by example, leave a similar legacy to my children.

These days you often tell me I should be slowing down, and I agree – just how to, I have not yet worked out. (That's not something you showed me by example!) But I am working towards enjoying more time with all who are dear to me, and spending more time in theatres, jazz clubs, etc. as a patron rather than a person visiting a workplace, and making sure not to miss our regular Sunday afternoon Happy Hour drinks and chips.

With thanks and love,

Neil

Neil Croker: entertainment and events producer

Dear Dad

You were born to be a father to daughters. You knew every word of every song from *The Little Mermaid, Beauty and the Beast, Aladdin* and ABBA. You would plait our hair, wash our clothes, cook our meals, take us to ballet, and prepare our school lunches (although, if I'm being picky, you always cut the tomato, cheese and polony way too thick). You were the primary carer in the '90s; a time when it was quite unusual for a man to bear the brunt of the load at home.

You left a secure job that you resented to pursue your passion, writing. A decision that I feel conflicted about. Conflicted because of my loyalty to Mum, knowing the hardship and pressure this decision caused her and the time she spent away from us, and the subsequent pain and guilt she carries about it. Conflicted, because on the flip side I also feel proud that you made that decision to follow your dreams. Conflicted because, 30 years later, I am now a freelancer, with a young family. Am I putting that same financial pressure on my husband? Is it different because I, the primary carer, am female? It shouldn't be. I have left jobs that made me miserable to pursue my passion, to seek out work that lights up my soul. I think I had the courage to do this because I had seen you do the same.

You always filled our days with music, games, stories, make-believe and laughter. Because there was no love in your marriage, you each poured every fibre of love and joy you had into us, and selflessly lived for us. Twenty years later you have both moved on and are happy with other people, and we can all still hang out as one happy, modern family. For that, I will be forever grateful to you both.

So, in the words of ABBA, thank you for the music ... And in the words of Ariel from *The Little Mermaid*, I love you Daddy.

Love your number-one fan,

Annaliese x

Annaliese Dent: podcaster and ambassador for the charity Rafiki Mwema

Dear Dad

It is sixteen years since you left, gave that final deep sigh and faded into yourself and that other place we often wonder about. And about 47 years since I first told you I would no longer call you Dad, but Stan, because that was your name and I wanted to know who you were, the whole you, not just the Dad bit.

And we made it happen, talked the talk I wanted when I was fifteen, but you were not ready. Can you remember that first conversation? You were pulling the blinds away to reveal the Indian Ocean that stretched all the way to everywhere, when you turned and said, 'What was I like as a father?' And I replied with words of truth that made you laugh: 'You were a prick, Stan, but you got better and that's why we're talking now.'

It all ended when the melanoma took your body and, slowly, your brain, and left you anxious, irritable and sometimes brutal, the kind of man I knew in my youth.

Or so I thought.

In secret you penned a letter that made grown men cry and women say, 'If only all fathers could leave such letters to their sons.'

You wrote why you never said you loved us, respected us or were proud of us, because men of your generation didn't say such things. Then you wrote of your love, respect and pride and you thanked us for being your sons and showing you new ways to be a father.

Stan, you may have left, but you live on in all of us.

Jon

Jon Doust: comedian, writer and speaker

Dear Dad

This is your firstborn who has idolised you her whole life and is now in despair as your photographic memory, high intelligence, perfect recollections and big, big love slowly fade away, squeezed into a darkness by a disease that cripples and overwhelms both of us.

I wish I was closer. I wish I could bring you back into focus just by holding your hand or stroking your face. Am I being insensitive by not being there? Does it make a difference?

I'm pretty sure I scared the pants off Mum when I was born – she was so sick and I was so tiny. Happily we both survived, but I'm not sure I gave Mum much confidence … bathing me in the Mixmaster bowl at 3 lbs 4 oz would've been scary! But fourteen months later my healthier sister arrived, and Mum was happy.

I was so drawn to you, Dad. You were my hero and I have a lifetime of wonderful memories. You made me feel brave and protected as I stormed through snake-infested bush to get to our secret crabbing spot. Just me and you. Or sitting in the passenger seat as you slowly drove, teaching me about the stars while we searched for fallen telephone lines after a huge storm in the dead of night. Just me and you.

And I remember the first time I heard the Beach Boys' 'Good Vibrations' ... just me and you. You thought it was time to have 'the sex talk'. I pretended I was listening to you but my fourteen-year-old self wanted to melt into the seat. That song brings it all back every time.

Now that I'm a parent and grandparent, I want to thank you for being such a great role model.

Love you and miss you, Dad,

Sooz

Sue Camilleri: band manager, national publicist

Dear Dad

Did I tell you I've been published? Because I have. Seriously. Ask Mum. Ask Samuel Johnson. Ask the actual book you're holding right now. And maybe tell me how impressed and proud of me you are. I dunno, whatever, it's not like I'm craving approval from my father or anything! Geez, Dad, I'm not one of *those* sons, ha ha.

It is a lot to take in, though. I'm published now. Objectively, it's a really big deal. And no doubt you have some questions. So, let's answer those first.

- No, I wasn't paid. (It's for charity.)
- No, Samuel Johnson doesn't now 'owe me one'.
- Yes, I wrote it by myself.
- And yes, a *proper* writer proofread it before it was published.

When Samuel Johnson (THE Samuel Johnson) asked me to contribute to this beautiful book, of course I said yes. But I had no idea what I would write. So, I sat down, put pen to paper, and was immediately reminded that I own a computer so started typing on that instead.

Obviously I said yes because it was for charity. I knew that'd reflect very favourably on my perceived compassion and generosity with the general public. It also presented an opportunity to exhibit my unique prose and ability to play with form in a subversive way. For charity.

Then it hit me. This isn't about *me*. It's about *you*. I should probably include a bit about how I love you and how I never take you for granted and how you've given me a life I'm only now starting to truly appreciate and be grateful for. But even though I know I *should* put all that in, I'm just not sure how to make it funny yet.

Happy Father's Day,

Ryan

Ryan Shelton: comedian, actor and mixed netball player

Dear Dad

You're a menace and I love you.

Thank you for not bubble-wrapping me and for filling my childhood with near-death experiences. Through your 'she'll be right' attitude towards parenting, I think you inadvertently taught me resilience.

Thank you for that time you built a flying fox off the ten-metre-high cliffs into the ocean and got me to 'try it out' (resulting in a Wile E. Coyote–style boulder incident). Thank you for the water fights when you used to fill the fire extinguisher with water and pressurise it using the car engine and then use SWOT riot techniques on all the children. And thank you for that time you took me to feed rabbits on a farm (years later revealing that we actually fed the hundreds of rabbits 1080 poison).

All of these dangerous childhood moments taught me to roll with the punches. I always bounced back because, despite the fact that you were reckless, you were generous with love, laughter and support. I never once doubted myself because you always said, 'Give it a go.' Even if that was jumping off a cliff or driving a car on the beach at ten years of age.

By not bubble-wrapping me you taught me to believe in myself and not fear taking a gamble. You showed me that even though things go wrong, we can laugh at them, rebuild the flying fox and then try jumping again.

I adore you, buddy, always have, always will.

Amy

Amy Hetherington: terminally positive comedian and writer

Acknowledgements

Dear Santa, I couldn't have done this without you. If not for the success of *Dear Santa, Dear Dad* would never have happened. So, I reluctantly dedicate this acknowledgement to Santa. Father Christmas is probably a dad, after all. Must be. How else did he get his title? Moving on.

I'm marked as editor on the cover. I didn't edit this. I didn't have the time. And I'm not an editor ... Jacquie Brown was the editor. Not on the cover, but here in the acknowledgements which hopefully no one reads. Sue Camilleri sourced many of these letters, and Jacinta Waters from Creative Representation had a good crack at it too. To all of our contributors, thank you for your time, for your brainwords, and for donating your letters free of charge. Thanks to Shaun Tan for the critters, to Chris Maddigan for lending a hand, to Vanessa Radnidge who continues to try her best, and to Lucy Freeman who worked tirelessly on this book and now wishes she was dead.

Righto. That'll do.

loveyoursister.org